W9-BYS-731

MULTICULTURAL EDUCATION SERIES

James A. Banks, Series Editor

(continued)

Our Worlds in Our Words

EXPLORING RACE, CLASS, GENDER, AND SEXUAL ORIENTATION IN MULTICULTURAL CLASSROOMS

TOURO COLLEGE LIBRARY
Kings Hwy

Mary Dilg

WITHDRAWN

TEACHERS COLLEGE PRESS

Teachers College, Columbia University
New York and London

KH

Published by Teachers College Press, 1234 Amsterdam Avenue, New York, NY 10027

Copyright © 2010 by Teachers College, Columbia University

All rights reserved. No part of this publication may be reproduced or transmitted in any form or by any means, electronic or mechanical, including photocopy, or any information storage and retrieval system, without permission from the publisher.

Library of Congress Cataloging-in-Publication Data

Dilg, Mary.
  Our worlds in our words : exploring race, class, gender, and sexual orientation in multicultural classrooms / Mary Dilg.
      p.   cm. — (Multicultural education series)
  Includes bibliographical references and index.
  ISBN 978-0-8077-5116-9 (pbk : alk. paper) — ISBN 978-0-8077-5117-6 (cloth : alk. paper)
    1. Multicultural education—United States.   2. Race relations—United States.
3. Minorities—Education—United States.   4. Sexual minority students—Education—United States.   I. Title.

  LC1099.3.D545 2010
  370.1170973—dc22

                                                                    2010021422

ISBN: 978-0-8077-5116-9 (paper)
ISBN: 978-0-8077-5117-6 (cloth)

Printed on acid-free paper
Manufactured in the United States of America

17 16 15 14 13 12 11 10   8 7 6 5 4 3 2 1

10/4/11

For Fennie Curry and Elsa Baehr:
For the life of the heart and the life of the mind,
I hear your voices still

Contents

Series Foreword

This book is a source of inspiration and hope in these challenging and dispiriting times in which many publications about schools are discouraging. Readers absorb the words of a gifted, caring, and insightful teacher who is a master of her craft in this timely and practical book. Dilg has deep subject matter knowledge and rich pedagogical skills that enable her to engage students in sophisticated and challenging content about diversity in their lives, in school, and in the United States. Dilg's thick ethnographic descriptions of her interactions with students and her skillful questioning reveal that she has a clarified and reflective philosophical stance on how to prepare students to live in a diverse society stratified by race, class, and gender.

Dilg has a discerning ethnographic eye that enables her to provide vivid and engaging descriptions of students framing complicated analyses and giving emotional responses to literary selections, autobiographical accounts, films, and scholarly essays. The reader observes students developing deep understandings of intricate issues related to race, class, gender, and sexual orientation. These rich and deeply textured ethnographic descriptions provide classroom teachers and teacher educators with graphic examples of how to engage students with rich content that teaches students important ideas about diversity and that evokes intense student intellectual and emotional responses.

A linchpin of this illuminating and visionary book is how Dilg illustrates with telling examples how content about diversity can be used to teach students the basic and higher level literacy and social science analysis skills that are essential for students to perform successfully on standardized tests and to succeed in life. Dilg makes it explicit how knowledge about race, class, gender, and sexual orientation that touches the lives of students, evokes powerful responses from them, and helps them to understand their personal journeys is a strong source of motivation to learn. With lively examples of students' engagement with and mastery of diversity content, Dilg belies the entrenched and pervasive notion that teaching and learning about diversity is an impediment to students' acquisition of the basic and higher level skills that are tested on standardized tests.

The approaches to teaching multicultural content described by Dilg will help teachers deal effectively with the growing ethnic, cultural, and linguistic diversity within the United States and the schools. American classrooms are experiencing the largest influx of immigrant students since the beginning of the 20th century. About a million immigrants are making the United States their home each year (Martin & Midgley, 1999). Between 1997 and 2006, 9,105,162 immigrants entered the United States (U.S. Department of Homeland Security, 2007). Only 15% came from nations in Europe. Most came from nations in Asia, from Mexico, and from nations in Latin America, Central America, and the Caribbean (U.S. Department of Homeland Security, 2007). A large but undetermined number of undocumented immigrants also enter the United States each year. In 2007, the *New York Times* estimated that there were 12 million illegal immigrants in the United States ("Immigration Sabotage," 2007). The influence of an increasingly ethnically diverse population on U.S. schools, colleges, and universities is and will continue to be enormous.

Schools in the United States are more diverse today than they have been since the early 1900s, when a multitude of immigrants entered the United States from Southern, Central, and Eastern Europe. In the 34-year period between 1973 and 2007, the percentage of students of color in U.S. public schools increased from 22 to 55% (Dillon, 2006; National Center for Education Statistics, 2008c). If current trends continue, students of color will equal or exceed the percentage of White students in U.S. public schools within one or two decades. In the 2007–2008 school year, students of color exceeded the number of White students in 11 states: Arizona, California, Florida, Georgia, Hawaii, Louisiana, Maryland, Mississippi, New Mexico, Nevada, and Texas (National Center for Education Statistics, 2008a, 2008b).

Language and religious diversity is also increasing in the U.S. student population. In 2000, about 20% of the school-age population spoke a language at home other than English (U.S. Census Bureau, 2003). The Progressive Policy Institute (2008) estimated that 50 million Americans (out of 300 million) spoke a language at home other than English in 2008. Harvard professor Diana L. Eck (2001) calls the United States the "most religiously diverse nation on earth" (p. 4). Islam is now the fastest-growing religion in the United States, as well as in several European nations, such as France, the United Kingdom, and The Netherlands (Banks, 2009; Cesari, 2004). Most teachers now in the classroom and in teacher education programs are likely to have students from diverse ethnic, racial, linguistic, and religious groups in their classrooms during their careers. This is true for both inner city and suburban teachers in the United States and as in many other Western nations (Banks, 2009).

The major purpose of the Multicultural Education Series is to provide preservice educators, practicing educators, graduate students, scholars, and policymakers with an interrelated and comprehensive set of books that summarizes and analyzes important research, theory, and practice related to the education of ethnic, racial, cultural, and linguistic groups in the United States and the education of mainstream students about diversity. The dimensions of multicultural education, developed by Banks (2004) and described in the *Handbook of Research on Multicultural Education,* provide the conceptual framework for the development of the publications in the series. Those dimensions are *content integration, the knowledge construction process, prejudice reduction, an equity pedagogy,* and *an empowering school culture and social structure.*

The books in the series provide research, theoretical, and practical knowledge about the behaviors and learning characteristics of students of color, language minority students, and low-income students. They also provide knowledge about ways to improve academic achievement and race relations in educational settings. Multicultural education is consequently as important for middle-class White suburban students as it is for students of color who live in the inner city. Multicultural education fosters the public good and the overarching goals of the commonwealth.

An important aim of Dilg's project is to educate students who will be effective citizens in a multicultural nation and world. She describes and illustrates why it is essential to help students acquire the knowledge, attitudes, and skills needed to cross cultural borders, to view the United States and the world from the perspectives of different racial, cultural, and gender groups, and to develop a commitment to act to make our nation and world more democratic and just.

We are fortunate that Dilg shares the teaching and learning that occurs in her intellectually stimulating classroom in this useful and luminous book. Her descriptions enable readers to experience her gifts and insights that benefit her students each day. Educators will be enriched and edified by reading this lucid and trenchant book. I am grateful to Dilg for once again writing a book for the Multicultural Education Series that integrates her incisive mind, compassion, deep content knowledge, and the pedagogical skills of a master teacher.

—James A. Banks

REFERENCES

Banks, J. A. (2004). Multicultural education: Historical development, dimensions, and practice. In J. A. Banks & C.A.M. Banks (Eds.), *Handbook of research on multicultural education* (2nd ed., pp. 3–29). San Francisco: Jossey-Bass.

Banks, J. A. (Ed.). (2009). *The Routledge international companion to multicultural education.* New York and London: Routledge.

Cesari, J. (2004). *When Islam and democracy meet: Muslims in Europe and the United States.* New York: Pelgrave Macmillan.

Dillon, S. (2006, August 27). In schools across U.S., the melting pot overflows. *New York Times,* pp. A7 & 16.

Eck, D. L. (2001). *A new religious America: How a "Christian country" has become the world's most religiously diverse nation.* New York: HarperSanFrancisco.

Immigration sabotage [Editorial]. (2007, June 4). *New York Times,* p. A22.

Martin, P., & Midgley, E. (1999). Immigration to the United States. *Population Bulletin, 54*(2), pp. 1–44. Washington, DC: Population Reference Bureau.

National Center for Education Statistics. (2008a). *The condition of education 2008.* Washington, DC: U.S. Department of Education. Retrieved August 26, 2009, from http://nces.ed.gov/pubsearch/pubsinfo.asp?pubid=2008031

National Center for Education Statistics. (2008b). *Public elementary/secondary school universe survey, 2007–2008: Common core of data.* Retrieved January 20, 2010, from http://nces.ed.gov/ccd

National Center for Education Statistics. (2008c). *State nonfiscal survey of public elementary/secondary education, 2007–2008: Common core of data.* Retrieved January 20, 2010, from http://nces.ed.gov/ccd

Progressive Policy Institute. (2008). *Fifty million Americans speak languages other than English at home.* Retrieved September 2, 2008, from http://www.ppionline.org/ppi_ci.cfm?knlgAreaID=108&subsecID=900003&contentID=254619

U.S. Census Bureau. (2003, October). *Language use and English-speaking ability: 2000.* Retrieved September 2, 2008, from http://www.census.gov/prod/2003pubs/c2kbr-29.pdf

U.S. Department of Homeland Security. (2007). *Yearbook of immigration statistics, 2006.* Washington, DC: Author, Office of Immigration Statistics. Retrieved August 11, 2009, from http://www.dhs.gov/files/statistics/publications/yearbook.shtm

Acknowledgments

For Jonathan Marks, president of the Board of Trustees; Kay Grossman, former president; John Levi, former president; members of the Board of Trustees; and parents of the Francis W. Parker School in Chicago for supporting an education grounded in the needs of both children and society, and an environment where faculty members can spend a lifetime in growth and discovery.

For Daniel Frank, principal of the Francis W. Parker School, for modeling and sustaining, each day, a belief in education grounded in progressive principles; and for saying, each time, "You can do that."

For Robert Merrick, historian, teacher, colleague, and friend, for showing me what was possible in a classroom.

For Joe Ruggiero, head of the Upper School; Michael Mahany, chairman of the English Department; and Andrew Bigelow, faculty member of the History Department of the Francis W. Parker School, for supporting this thinking, teaching, and writing.

For colleagues and friends who create every day in a school, a world that nurtures a caring and thoughtful engagement with ideas among adults and students.

For my students, whose wisdom, perspectives, and generosity of spirit fill these pages.

For James Banks, Kerry and Linda Killinger Professor of Diversity Studies, director of the Center for Multicultural Education at the University of Washington–Seattle, and editor of the Multicultural Education Series at Teachers College Press, whose vision, leadership, and lifetime of selfless hard work have moved a nation toward a more just and essential form of education.

For Brian Ellerbeck, executive acquisitions editor of Teachers College Press, whose understanding of the nature and direction of education in this country, wisdom about teaching and learning and writing, and ability to give supportive and specific guidance as editor made this book possible.

For each of the professional and caring members of the publishing team at Teachers College Press who brought this book into being.

For my family, Russ, Aynsley, and Justin Vandenbroucke and Mathew Pokoik, for their selfless support of a wife, mother, and mother-in-law, who, beyond her family, also loved to teach, to read, and to write.

A Note on Usage

The whole of this text is meant to be inclusive of gay, lesbian, bisexual, and transgender individuals, couples, and families. For the sake of brevity, and an uneasiness with using simply the letters GLBT as a designation for a multitude of rich and complex lives, references to "gays and lesbians," "gay and lesbian couples," or "gay and lesbian families" should be taken to be inclusive of bisexual and transgender individuals, couples, and families as well.

Honoring High Standards: Reading, Writing, Speaking, and Listening in a Multicultural Classroom

CONTEXT

In an era of increasing diversity, a critical need for literacy among our students, and a broadening need for supporting life in a multicultural society, this book offers a glimpse into two high school English courses in a 100-year-old, independent, progressive JK–12 school serving a diverse student population in Chicago. All of the following chapters describe teaching literature, writing, and communication in ways that acknowledge the identity and needs of each student, place the student and his or her passion for learning at the center of classroom life; embrace multiple forms of assessment; and are broadly consistent with multiple states' standards for English language arts as well as for multicultural education. They reflect an expansive curriculum through which these students learn to read, to write, to think, and, through sharing their ideas and concerns with one another, to build a sustaining multicultural community in the classroom.

The two courses through which I know and work with these students include a year-long required course on literary genres for freshmen and a semester-long elective course on issues of race, culture, class, gender, and sexual orientation for juniors and seniors. Both attempt to honor the complexity of students and their yearning to understand their world. Both courses embrace a broad, inclusive, and demanding curriculum, one that reflects the students' world and helps to equip them for that world, whatever they wish to pursue within it. They reflect a form of learning that is at once rigorous and supportive, based on developing skills that prepare students to read the world, to write the world, and to build workable relationships and communities within that world.

The students in this classroom become astute readers by reading; become effective writers by writing; and become thoughtful communicators through discussions, presentations, and community building in their multicultural classroom. Their assessments are based on their writing of scripts, poetry, fiction, nonfiction, journal entries, analytical essays, and essay exams; through their creating of multimedia and digital projects; through their formal and informal presentations; and through the ways in which they enter into dialogues with one another about works of literature and films and the issues about life around them that those works raise.*

In Reading and Writing Across the Genres: Self and Community, a year-long required course for freshmen, students read and discuss works of literature, classic and contemporary, focusing on evolving individuals within the contexts of home, family, community, the natural world, and personal quests, and experiment with developing their own voices as writers. The first semester focuses on works for the stage, poetry, and the 19th-century novel; the second semester explores the 20th-century novel, short fiction, nonfiction, and writing in a digital environment. Works studied include George Bernard Shaw's *Pygmalion*, August Wilson's *Fences*, and David Henry Hwang's *FOB*; the work of over 30 poets from multiple eras and cultures; Lewis Carroll's *Alice in Wonderland*, Kurt Vonnegut's *Slaughterhouse-Five*, and Sandra Cisneros's *The House on Mango Street*; the short fiction of African American, Latina/o American, Asian American, Native American, Jewish American, bicultural, and White American writers, as well as writers known for their work in the personal essay and nonfiction. Students write analytical essays; scenes for the stage; poetry; character sketches; vignettes; short stories; interdisciplinary research papers bringing together perspectives from multiple disciplines on a single aspect of human experience; and digital autobiographies or biographies, weaving together original nonfiction narratives, images, and sound in a five-minute film using iMovie (Appendix A).

Issues of Race, Class, Gender, and Sexual Orientation, a semester-long elective course for juniors and seniors, enables students to examine issues emerging from multiple self-identified groups, as well as overarching issues, through the work of contemporary scholars, writers, and artists; to discuss these significant issues with one another across lines that often divide us; and to write about the issues. Writers include, among others, Arturo Madrid, Cherríe Moraga, June Jordan, Ronald Takaki, bell hooks, Richard Rodriguez, Helena Maria Viramontes, Cornel West, Toni Morrison, Frank Chin, Art Spiegelman, and Bernard Malamud, as well as those within anthologies of gay and lesbian writers, bicultural writers, and Arab American writers. Films include *School Colors*, *Children of the Harvest*, *Tortilla Soup*, *Bamboozled*, *A Strong Clear Vision*, *The Cats of Mirikitani*, *Sophie's Choice*, *The Wedding Banquet*, *An American Love Story*, *Mississippi Masala*, *Planet of the Arabs*, *Brothers and Others*; videos from YouTube; and *Crash*. The syllabus for this course is constantly evolving in response to student needs and emerging issues in American life. Early years of the course

---

*Copies of syllabi and writing assignments for both courses, cited throughout as Appendix A or Appendix B, are available online (http://www.tcpress.com).

included a major segment on Native American writers and issues, including the study of Leslie Marmon Silko's novel *Ceremony*. Over the years, segments have been added on the lives and issues of bicultural Americans; Arab Americans; gay, lesbian, bisexual, and transgender Americans; and on issues of socioeconomic class (Appendix B).

OVERVIEW

The chapters that follow take us into the work of students in each of these courses. Chapter 1 frames the work of both courses in the context of the realities of these students' society and the need to have all students achieve high standards in reading, writing, speaking, listening, and research. Chapters 2, 3, and 4 take the reader into classes in Issues of Race, Class, Gender, and Sexual Orientation. We see students reading and responding to the works of scholars, writers, and filmmakers grappling, respectively, with aspects of race, culture, and gender; class; and sexual orientation through the lens of multiple cultures. Chapter 5 describes teaching writing through an approach that begins with students reading significant works of literature across multiple genres and cultures, and with the students' own needs as thinkers and writers. Readers will see freshmen writers making art, and they will see juniors and seniors writing for journals and writing analytical essays. Chapter 6 returns to Issues of Race, Class, Gender, and Sexual Orientation course and enables readers to see the process and explore the implications of building a multicultural community in the classroom. Throughout, readers will hear the voices of students through their participation in discussions and through their writing. Identifying details of students, except for a broad cultural identity, have been changed to protect their privacy.

Chapter 1, "Contemporary Society, Standards, and a Passion for Learning in a Multicultural World," provides a context and rationale for the teaching and learning described throughout these pages. In a complex society often divided by issues tied to race, class, gender, or sexual orientation, there is a crucial need for students to gain skills for literacy as well as skills for supporting a healthy, diverse democracy. This chapter examines the process of educating for skills and educating for meaning in a multicultural society within the context of three questions: Why should teachers who are faced with standards and accountability deal with multicultural content? To what extent are the learning of skills and the learning of multicultural content compatible? How can teachers who are faced with the push to increase students' scores on standardized tests use multicultural content to attain these scores?

Chapter 2, "Exploring Race, Culture, and Gender Through American Literature and Films: Understanding Self and Others," enables the reader to journey across America with students as they examine issues of race, culture, and gender in the works of Latino American, Asian American, African American, Jewish American, Arab American, and biracial writers, artists, and scholars. Through such broad-based reading, students explore factors that bring us together or drive us apart, as well as factors that support or inhibit the lives of men and women. Beyond acquainting students with well-known and emerging writers from the multiple literary traditions that make up the literature of America, this course became one of the first in the country to adopt a newly published collection of Arab American writers of short fiction, *Dinarzad's Children*, a text grounded in the real and varied lives of Arab Americans and therefore offering students crucial counternarratives to the misinformation flooding the media about Arab Americans after September 11, 2001. Educator Pauline Lipman (2004) reminds us that such teaching and learning is "an urgent necessity if students are to survive and challenge deepening global social chasms of class, gender, race, and ethnicity" (p. 167).

Chapter 3, "Reading Literature and Films Through the Lens of Class: Breaking Taboos, Examining Factors That Influence Class Membership and Mobility," describes students exploring texts and films through the lens of socioeconomic class. Each of the lives in these works provides a glimpse in one way or another into the factors that influence class membership in America, factors that allow individuals to move toward the gilded American Dream or bind them to a life of restricted opportunities, an endless financial precariousness with little hope of change. Readings and discussions that explore the nature and impact of class in American lives enable these students to come together across class lines to learn about and debate this aspect of their lives. In so doing, they experience what Jane Van Galen (2007) urges educators to consider: "schooling in which class stratification is named but not reproduced . . . education in which poor, working class, and more privileged students all come to better understand how social class has been at the very core of their imaginations of who they might be and become" (p. 12), an engagement with one another important for these students' futures and for ours.

Chapter 4, "Gay, Lesbian, Bisexual, and Transgender Lives and Issues, Readings and Films: Countering Invisibility, Interrupting the Cycle of Homophobia," follows students as they explore lives and issues of gay, lesbian, bisexual, and transgender individuals and families through classic and contemporary literature and films, as well as scholarly essays. Shifting attitudes toward aspects of gender, sexual orientation, and family life can confuse students and complicate their coming together in a classroom. The reader will see in this classroom an opportunity and a safe environment for all students to learn more about these aspects of American life: to raise their questions, explore their confusions, and share their perspectives. Such study is consistent with what Arthur Lipkin (1999), educator and founder of the Gay and Lesbian School Issues Project, suggests should take place in schools: "What is needed in antihomophobia education is sustained and serious discourse within the disciplines of the school" (p. 341).

Chapter 5, "Writing for Self and Others, Writing for Life: Speaking to Journals, Making Art, Building Arguments," invites the reader into a classroom where respect for young writers, a trusting environment, and the freedom for these young writers to write what they need to write results in good writing, day after day. These students learn to write—and meet high standards of writing—by being writers. We see them writing for course journals; creating scripts, poetry, fiction, and nonfiction; working in traditional and digital modes; and building arguments through which to persuade their audience about ideas central to their thinking on crucial issues. We also see them writing within a context that supports them in an ever more salient aspect of writing in this nation: writing for a multicultural audience. Their work stands as testament to the beauty and the thoughtfulness of students' writing as it emerges in an atmosphere of freedom and support and without standardized testing as a measure of success.

Chapter 6, "A Multicultural Classroom: A Real and Precious Community," examines the process by which students in a multicultural classroom move from the relative isolation of their own lives, cultures, identity groups, neighborhoods, and perspectives to feeling part of a multicultural community. As students share their responses to readings and films, they move from being a random gathering of individuals who have come together across significant divides to being a closer and more caring group, more invested in the lives, perspectives, and needs of one another. The community we establish in the multicultural classroom is an important step for the next steps of these students' lives and for their future communities. This chapter positions such community building within the context of cross-cultural dynamics in the history of American schooling, the power of reconceiving the notion of cultural capital in the classroom, and the usefulness of skills in multicultural community building in the next settings of these students' lives.

OF STUDIES AND COMMUNITIES, STANDARDS AND POSSIBILITIES

I invite you to join my students as they read, discuss, and write about their world; as they explore individual lives and communities in part influenced by identities tied to race, culture, class, gender, or sexual orientation; and, through sharing their own emerging perspectives, build a nurturing, viable, and vital multicultural community within their classroom. To create an environment that supports each student's journey of discovery while fostering a community of learners enables both teachers and students to engage in some of the most exciting work in an American classroom while respecting the most exacting of standards.

There will be readers, perhaps, who question the thrust of this broad social context for the study of literature and writing. But is it not the intention of each of these writers to offer his or her reader some form of insight into our complex world? Additionally, nestling the study of literature and writing within the context of films, research, and theories broadens students' interpretive skills, opens up multiple dimensions of these works of literature, and deepens students' understanding of multiple modes of writing. Such study embraces the work of writers, artists, and scholars who hold dreams of a better life for all, offer insight to their hungry readers, and engage students in issues of their times.

The teaching and learning described in these chapters emerges within a school that is able to support well its educational mission, and that support makes possible much of what happens there. With our nation bending under the effects of more than a century of unequal educational opportunities for our children, however, is it not time to make the nature and level of resources for all of our schools commensurate with our long-standing status as one of the richest nations in the world and provide equal educational opportunities for all of our students? The observations offered in the pages that follow are offered in a belief in the necessity of that happening.

CHAPTER 1

Contemporary Society, Standards, and a Passion for Learning in a Multicultural World

This union may never be perfect, but generation after generation has shown that it can always be perfected. And today, whenever I find myself feeling doubtful or cynical about this possibility, what gives me the most hope is the next generation.

—Barack Obama, "A More Perfect Union"

INTRODUCTION

On a summer day in 2008, Senator and Reverend James Meeks, a Black Illinois state senator and Chicago minister, called for all public school students of Chicago not to report for school on the first day of the coming academic year. Instead, in a form of demonstration, they would be bused to legendary New Trier High School in the affluent suburb of Winnetka—and to other well-funded suburban schools—to register for classes (WLS-TV, 2008). The city of Winnetka pays almost double what the city of Chicago pays to educate each of its students. The next morning, David Brooks (2008), a White moderate conservative columnist for *The New York Times* cautioned:

> The skills slowdown [for America's students] is the biggest issue facing the country. This threatens the country's long-term prospects. It also widens the gap between rich and poor. This slow-moving problem, more than any other, will shape the destiny of the nation. (p. A19)

That spring, Gary Orfield (2008), a professor and co-director of the Civil Rights Project/Proyecto Derechos Civiles, University of California–Los Angeles, had written:

> We are a nation where the White population will become the minority in the nation's schools in just a few years. American parents, by very large majorities, want their children to grow up understanding how to relate successfully with all groups in a diverse society. Addressing these issues isn't a luxury or an optional part of education. It goes to the core of what makes our schools and communities work. (p. 1)

7

These moments are not unrelated. Together they lay out critical goals for an American system of education that, for over a century, has been more successful at funding and educating some students than others and in which neighborhood schools segregated by race and by class offer little chance for students to know each other across lines of race, culture, or class. What James Meeks, David Brooks, and Gary Orfield speak to is a three-pronged goal for American education: adequate funding and educational opportunities to equip all of our students with skills for sustaining this long running democracy—as well as skills for supporting diverse communities. This book emerged within the context of these evolving directions for the future of American schools.

The society in which these students grow and flourish is the same society that often threatens their growth, freedom, possibility, and well-being through ongoing racism, sexism, deep divisions by class, and homophobia. It is a society that tends to push students ever farther apart rather than bring them together. Those upon whom society has placed significant challenges tied to race, culture, gender, class, or sexual orientation must sometimes struggle to find healthy reflections of their lives in their studies, as well as opportunities and power. And those upon whom society has showered multiple privileges increasingly grow up isolated from others. In the face of that reality, we need to establish a focus and an environment in our classrooms in which all of our students can see their own lives and the lives of others in their studies, and engage in the process of sorting out the larger world they inherit. We need to help them envision a place for themselves in that world, help them take steps that will move them successfully toward that future, and help them to do so with the cognizance of the needs of others and the ways in which they can act on that knowledge. American scholars, writers, and filmmakers—the literature and art of America—can help us do that.

In the study of American literature, there has always been a parallel between groups discriminated against in society and the literature read in the classroom. Attitudes on the part of the dominant population toward people of color, women, and the poor, as well as gays and lesbians, has led to the exclusion and silencing of many writers for generations and to the bifurcation of identity for many others, as gay and lesbian authors are often taught divorced from their identity as gay or lesbian. This in turn has diminished the opportunity for many students to find themselves in the literature they read and for others to read beyond the confines of their own cultures and learn, crucially, of the lives of others. Such practices have impeded students from discovering and knowing the essential multicultural nature of American literature. Helena Maria Viramontes, winner of the John Dos Passos Prize for Literature and the Luis Leal Award for Distinction in Chicano/Latino Literature and a professor of English at Cornell University, recalls leaving an MFA program at the University of California–Irvine because a professor was critical of her for focusing on Chicanos in her writing (Shea, 2007). Similar attitudes on the part of White teachers and academics have dominated literature classrooms for many decades, despite the essentially multicultural nature of this country and its literature. All of our students should be educated in the essential nature of American literature. All of our students have the right to know that there are myriad powerful works that speak to their own worlds and myriad powerful works that take them into the worlds of others—to illuminate their day-to-day lives, to answer their questions, to give them a broader understanding of lives in a multicultural society.

Perhaps never in our history have we educators and our students been surrounded by so much information and knowledge and, if David Brooks is right, has our nation been so threatened by an inadequate level of skills in our students.

In the face of these realities, our nation sorely needs to build communities of learners no longer segregated by unequal opportunities, by race and by class, and to ensure that all of our students can gain the skills necessary for them—and for our nation—to thrive. This book is a glimpse into one classroom in Chicago where students come together across many of the social, cultural, and economic lines that divide them, and, together, engage in reading, thinking, discussions, and writing; in developing those lifelong skills, they also build and nurture a multicultural community. In an often bleak landscape of significant educational challenges facing our families, our children, and our society, these students give me great hope.

COMING TOGETHER FROM A DIVIDED SOCIETY: DIVIDED NEIGHBORHOODS/DIVIDED LIVES

My students are Asian American, Latino American, African American, European American, Middle Eastern American, part Native American, biracial and multiethnic, and religiously diverse. They reflect differences in class. They are male and female, straight and gay. Most were born in this country; others have arrived in this country since their birth.

Many of these students have matured in largely racially and ethnically segregated neighborhoods that give rise to largely segregated neighborhood schools. They reflect the expansiveness, isolation, and tensions that accompany an increasingly multiracial society. They are a generation who will, in their adulthood, see the White majority replaced across America by a minority majority. Because this is an urban, progressive, tuition-based school that provides significant financial aid, and because it is a school that draws on many Chicago neighborhoods, the students in this classroom reflect a wider spectrum of racial and cultural backgrounds than do many classrooms today.

In this multicultural nation, classrooms that are broadly integrated across races and cultures are a shrinking phenomenon. Gary Orfield and John Yun (1999) explain in their ongoing study of school resegregation in America: "As the new century approaches we have become a far more racially and ethnically mixed nation, but in our schools, the color lines of increasing racial and ethnic separation are rising" (p. 5). Additionally, many schools forfeit opportunities for multicultural classrooms through academic tracking. Many of the original dreams of school integration have failed to materialize: Even within multicultural school populations, students often self-segregate. Further, the recent Supreme Court decision limiting the use of race by school districts to decide which students will attend which schools makes it even harder to create schools that will bring students together from diverse backgrounds and lives (Greenhouse, 2007).

This growing resegregation does not, in many ways, serve our students well. Orfield and Yun (1999) explain: "We are floating back toward an educational pattern that has never in the nation's history produced equal and successful schools" (p. 28). Beyond often stark differences in funding, opportunities, and achievement rates for schools serving populations that are predominantly students of color and schools serving populations that are predominantly White, such segregation of our students means that as our nation becomes more multicultural, our students have fewer opportunities to know well those whose lives are different from their own. And this, in turn, does not well serve our democracy.

Regardless of the neighborhoods that have surrounded each of these students, all of them have come of age in a racist society. Although surrounded by racism, these students have varying degrees of knowledge about racism and its workings. Far too many students have lived with the effects of racism all of their lives—it hovers over relationships, punctuates city bus rides, triggers fears of racial profiling or harassment, influences their daily choices and sense of possibilities; it affects how they see themselves and others and a sense of how others see them. Other students are much more removed from such moments. Although they hear and see racist moments around them, they have not been subjected to racism themselves. Thus, these students' identities and their daily lives have meant either an intimate relationship with race relations and racism or a more removed and distant understanding.

These students bring radically different experiences with race and radically different understandings of prejudice, discrimination, race relations, and racism into this classroom. Their varying lives and experiences have shaped their views and brought them to the shared moments in this classroom. They are tentative with each other. As studies have shown, in building friendships they gravitate toward those most similar to themselves. Their close relationships are often not broadly inclusive of those in other cultures or other socioeconomic classes.

Thus, even in the 21st century as the United States moves steadily toward a minority majority population, many students have little opportunity to know each other across racial or cultural lines in their largely segregated neighborhoods and schools. Additionally, their literature courses often offer little opportunity to know the breadth and richness of the truly multicultural literary tradition they inherit—the literary tradition within their own culture and the multiple literary traditions across the cultures that vitalize and define America today. They are deprived of hearing the voices and learning broadly of the America that surrounds them through these writers' voices. And this can handicap our students: "To continue the use of the current monocultural or bicultural curriculum is, therefore, tantamount to presenting students with information and facts about an obsolete worldview" (Sogunro, 2001, p. 21). The broad study of American writers reflected in the chapters that follow underscores the power of students connecting with texts and films that reflect their own and others' lives across multiple cultures. Such study addresses the hunger students have to read and to see works that help them interpret the world that they inhabit but that often confuses, limits, or isolates them.

The students in this classroom frame gender issues through their experiences thus far as young men and young women: what they have seen at home; in the media; in homes, neighborhoods, and communities beyond their own; and through the lives of their peers in this diverse school community. Some of these students view the world through a family in which men work and women stay home. Some come from families in which both parents are professionals. Some come from single-parent homes. And some come from homes in which parents work multiple jobs to sustain their families. Students bring to our forum widely diverging notions of the roles, expectations, possibilities, and challenges tied to men or women influenced by culturally based expectations of men and women; how the students see themselves; how others see them; stereotypes of men and women; the demands or opportunities life places before them; and their individual wishes and dreams.

Whatever cultural and gender dynamics students are aware of, researchers tell us that race, class, and gender still play powerful roles in the workplaces these students will inherit. According to Amott and Matthaei (1996), groups with little power occupy jobs "with lower pay, less job security, and more difficult and dangerous working conditions," and within workplaces, workers work in jobs segregated by race, gender, and class. Further, although in recent years Asian Americans have fared better than European Americans by a number of measures, and a small number of individuals from other groups of color have moved into jobs closed to them in the past, "men still earn much more than women, on average, as do Whites compared to non-Asian people of color." These authors conclude: "The very fact that so few who are not White men have made it to the top of the upper tier of the primary [labor] sector illustrates the pervasiveness of gender and race oppression" (pp. 318, 343, 347).

Examining lives nestled within specific cultural contexts invites a consideration of the multiple ways in which individuals define, interpret, or experience their identities as men or women. Works by writers, artists, and scholars reveal not only a wide variety of men's and women lives but also the opportunities and the challenges those men and women experience in a society in which dynamics based in race, culture, or gender still influence many men's and women's possibilities. For all of our students, it remains to be seen what opportunities for men and women—of color or White—will exist in what some optimistically call a postracial society inaugurated by the Obamas' move to the White House, a society these students now inherit.

If neighborhoods are often tied to a particular race or culture, they are also often linked to socioeconomic class. In an urban school drawing its student body from across a wide variety of city neighborhoods, class divisions follow students into the schoolroom. This means that although the students in front of me are in a small school and many of them have spent years in the same classes, they are, in some ways, strangers to each other. Many of these students have an awareness of multiple ways in which class affects their daily lives, but they have little opportunity to learn about the workings of class, especially as embodied in literature, and this leaves them grappling largely alone with the issues of class encircling their lives.

A lack of understanding of the impact of socioeconomic class on the lives of individuals and groups entrenches the status quo favoring those with economic power; further solidifies class boundaries; and prevents students from becoming more informed adults who can participate in public debates about issues, choices, and policies that affect their own and others' lives or to become agents of social change for economic justice. The study of literature provides an opportunity for all students to learn about the workings of class in many different types of lives in this country and for students across class lines to see their own lives reflected in the focus of their studies. Historically, reading lists have precluded that opportunity for many students (Linkon, 1999). Despite the broadening of the literary canon in recent years, reading lists are still overwhelmingly populated by White writers and few writers whose origins are in the working class.

Students are also caught in a vortex of shifting and contradictory attitudes toward gay, lesbian, bisexual, and transgender (GLBT) individuals and families. Nationally, as a culture we have moved from a period of silence to a period of open debate that lays bare not only the contemporary thrust toward recognizing equality and support for GLBT individuals and families but also continued open and violent rejection of them. Gay, lesbian, or transgender marriages and families in some areas flourish; in other areas, they are condemned. Gays and lesbians and gay and lesbian characters hold center stage in positive roles on television and in films. Transgender individuals have a "one in 12 chance of being murdered. In contrast, the average person has about a one in 18,000 chance of being murdered" (Human Rights Campaign, 2009). Educational researchers, psychologists, and social workers urge ending the silence around teaching about gay, lesbian, and transgender lives.

Within schools, gay, lesbian, bisexual, and transgender parents and parents of GLBT students call for more support for their children. Organizations such as the Gay, Lesbian, and Straight Education Network (GLSEN) and the Illinois Safe Schools Alliance take proactive roles in creating awareness of the need to support the lives of GLBT students in schools. Gay-straight-alliance organizations proliferate. Still, many gay, lesbian, bisexual, or transgender students are harassed or assaulted because of their sexual orientation. A gay eighth-grade student was shot to death by a classmate in the computer lab of their middle school in California (Cathcart, 2008). Most teachers begin teaching with little to no background in gay and lesbian history, literature, or issues and are reluctant to address them. Opposition to teaching about gay and lesbian lives prevents other teachers from broadening curricula. A student op-ed piece urging tolerance for gays in a high school newspaper in Indiana resulted in a 2-month suspension of the journalism teacher ("Teacher Suspended," 2007). Many gay teachers remain closeted for fear of their jobs. All of these factors send confusing, inaccurate, contradictory, and frightening messages to gay, lesbian, bisexual, and transgender students; students from gay-, lesbian-, bisexual-, and transgender-headed families; and straight students. They lack accurate information, knowledge, and understanding.

Thus, in matters of race, culture, gender, class, and sexual orientation, our students have questions about each other and each other's lives. They are aware of the many differences that tug them apart, but they may be uncertain about what has created connectedness or antipathies or distances among them. They may yearn to come together as a group, a class, or a multicultural school community. But their differences are often more powerful than their wishes or their needs to come together, and so, at times—like so many multicultural groups in America—they stumble along, bumping into one another across the lines that divide them and yearning for a closeness that remains elusive—an unattained vision of what could be. The divisions among them are real; their tentativeness is understandable.

As these students begin to share readings, films, dialogues, and writings in the classroom, however, they also begin to build a base of shared experiences. From their shared experiences emerge a shared language, history, frame of reference, and burgeoning trust. They begin to construct a new community with and for each other, a community where all of us can come together to learn of each other, to know better who we are, and to care about each other and each other's lives in this multicultural nation.

In an increasingly multicultural America with increasingly segregated schools, the mix in this classroom is an American Dream. It is the fulfillment of an American Dream of sorts on a long American journey—from multiple, long-running, and shameful attempts to keep students of color from gaining access to many of America's schools, to our being here together. And now, it is often a young version of America at its best.

EDUCATING FOR MEANING, EDUCATING FOR SKILLS IN A MULTICULTURAL SOCIETY

Beyond the complex social and cultural dynamics our students inherit in this multicultural society, the proliferation of texts and images on the Internet and readily available to many of our students both broadens and complicates their learning in a classroom. This emergent factor forces us as teachers to interrogate the meaning of reading and writing in our students' lives. If we are to be successful in inviting our students into a meaningful relationship with reading and writing in our classrooms, we need to understand something of the meaning of reading and writing in their lives. The encircling mass of texts and images this generation of students inherits reinvites us to think about the most basic uses of reading and writing in our lives.

We read out of a need for information, we read out of curiosity, or we read for delight. We read because we need to or because it brings us pleasure. Reading stimulates and facilitates problem solving, it gives us company, and it enables us to take on a sense of agency in our own lives. How can we as teachers tap into this ongoing robust need for reading in our students' lives? As Alfred Tatum (2005) has so presciently described in his *Teaching Reading to Black Adolescent Males*, the texts in our students' classrooms must be able to compete with the "texts" outside of their classrooms and to help them interpret the life that surrounds them.

In an information age, when students are flooded with data in multiple forms around the clock, and in an era when far too many students are confronted with the real "texts" of violence, poverty, loss, and a range of psychological pressures in their daily lives, what we offer our students in class must speak to their needs, their joys, and their lives. This year, over 30 school-age children have been murdered in Chicago. What relationship to reading will speak to the siblings and the friends of these children? When gangs have more power than the metropolitan police to control streets and neighborhoods, what relationship to reading will speak to these students? When family members lose jobs, and when housing in neighborhoods that families have lived in for generations is priced out of the reach of those families through gentrification, what relationship to reading will speak to these students? When students are being groomed to take their places in the global society and the global economy, what relationship to reading will speak to these children? Our students' relationship to reading inside a classroom must acknowledge, address, complement, and help students navigate all of the other "texts" of their lives. Only then will reading in our classrooms be able to compete with the texts surrounding these students outside of our rooms.

And yet, this is not broadly happening. State-sponsored reading lists in this multicultural nation remain overwhelmingly White (California Department of Education, 2004; New York State Education Department, 1997) and grounded in experiences at a far remove from many of our students' lives or the nature of their society. While all of us acknowledge the powerful and enduring ways in which literature can call to us across eras and cultures, we can also attest to its power when it speaks to us of our own worlds in ways that clarify those worlds and assist us in our daily lives. Research tells us that far too many teachers remain reluctant to bring in contemporary texts from multiple cultures. They remain unfamiliar with legions of stellar contemporary writers across the cultures that define the United States. They remain reluctant to give themselves broader education in these texts, and they remain reluctant to open their classrooms to discussions of the real, sensitive, and complex issues these artists and their works often address (Bigler & Collins, 1995). The result is that in too many classrooms, reading remains removed from the compelling experiences and texts that encircle our students. In our effort to teach them to read, we reduce reading to exercises using disembodied texts "interpreted" under the pressure of time. We are failing to show our students that reading texts can help them read their world (Freire, 1971). And so, we lose our students to the texts outside our classroom doors, texts unfolding on their sidewalks, on buses, in their neighborhoods, and in their handheld access to the Internet. We are fostering a growing disjuncture between their "learning" in school and their learning outside in their world.

But let us pose this same question about the role of writing in our lives. Again, our students are surrounded by writing, are indeed drowning in writing—in the visual cacophony of commercials that line their streets, the flood of screenwriting and writing for broadcast entering their lives through hundreds of channels of cable television, the growing number of texts on their iPods and cell phones, and the infinite forms of writing on the Internet. Simultaneously, the newspapers they or their parents have reached for each morning are dying, gasping and grasping for ways to survive beside the surfeit of writing on the Internet. Students' own experiences in learning to write in classrooms far too often culminate in fragmented and fragmenting questions—answered under the pressure of time—about disembodied texts far removed from the lives that beckon and intrude from just outside of our classroom doors. Students' "reward" for learning to write becomes a statistic for a school's "report card." In this environment, how can we help our students make meaning of writing—how can we support their learning to write as an extension of their daily interpretation and clarification of their lives? As with our approach to the teaching of reading, in the teaching of writing, we must return to the most essential relationship a writer has to writing: Writers turn to writing out of need—to clarify life around them, to clarify confusions within, to communicate a need, to further develop their thinking, to problem-solve, to reach out to another, to give pleasure to oneself and others, to make something of beauty and meaning. Engaged young writers are meaning makers making meaning of experience as they capture a moment, connect with another, or write to understand and persuade. We must support young writers in using writing to make meaning of their world and of their own lives in that world.

MEANINGFUL STANDARDS IN A DEMOCRATIC SOCIETY

All of these questions, of course, lead us to asking ourselves: How can we be effective teachers of reading and writing as well as ready our young charges to take their places in an increasingly complex democracy within the context of the society beyond our doors and the need to meet high standards within our doors? All good, thoughtful, effective teachers want their students to succeed. They want them to be able to read, to write, to think, to listen, and to speak clearly. These are the skills state standards embody. These are the skills that standardized tests address. These are also the skills at the center of classroom life described in the following chapters. The question becomes: How can we marry an education of meaning, an education for citizenship in our diverse democracy, with an education for essential skills? Why should teachers who are faced with standards and accountability deal with multicultural content? To what extent are the learning of skills and the learning of multicultural content compatible? And how can teachers faced with the push to increase students' scores on standardized tests use multicultural content to attain these scores?

Why Should Teachers Who Are Faced with Standards and Accountability Deal with Multicultural Content?

Multicultural texts and films are the texts and art of America. Perhaps even more significantly, literature and films emerging from across borders of race, class, gender, and sexual orientation give us a truth about the American experience rarely broadly portrayed in the literature of the historically dominant culture and thus present crucial perspectives for all of our students to know. To be educated in today's America is to have developed the capacity to evaluate circumstances and issues from multiple perspectives and to be able to move around more successfully in relation to borders of race, culture, class, gender, and sexual orientation. Such texts provide challenges and alternative points of view to narrower culture-of-origin perspectives and assumptions. They help our students develop both their minds and their hearts—the capacity for both critical thinking and empathy. They offer students the opportunity to become broad-minded citizens, to become more graceful and thoughtful citizens of a country and a democracy moving toward having no cultural majority.

More than ever before, texts offered students in schools must engage them. Texts emerging from multiple cultures have the power to do that. They are among the texts that can best compete and be in their own way as engaging to students as many of the "texts" beyond their schoolroom walls (Tatum, 2005). These works are responsive to their need to understand their world.

A vital connection between students and material stimulates analytical thinking, discussion, problem solving, and debate, not only about what they are reading but also about their own lives; and this in turn motivates students to embrace skills for reading, communication, and writing. Because these works emerge from and speak to multiple bases and forms of knowledge, they appeal to many types of learners, across multiple cultures. The result is that learning becomes compelling—and pleasurable. And pleasurable learning often leads to success for students, pride in their work, and a deepening relationship to learning. A focus on multicultural content for fostering skills in reading, communication, and writing ensures that the content for learning leading to assessment is meaningful and that preparing students for assessment is consistent with preparing students for living their lives.

A focus on multicultural content provides for an essential marriage of skills for literacy with skills for supporting life in a participatory multicultural democracy. Both sets of skills are crucial for 21st-century life. Students equipped with one set of skills but not the other will face disadvantages in a multicultural society. Thus, using multicultural texts and films to meet standards in reading, writing, speaking, and listening is responsive to our students' world and is best suited to provide them with skills for thriving in that world.

To What Extent Are the Learning of Skills and the Learning of Multicultural Content Compatible?

The work that I oversee each day with my own students suggests that teaching skills through a focus on multicultural texts and films offers students an education that is not only consistent with standards for English language arts but that goes beyond those standards.

The goals, the focus, and the process of learning in this classroom are broadly consistent with English language arts standards for reading, writing, speaking, and listening in New York State (New York State Education Department, 2005) and California (California State Board of Education, 2007); with the standards for reading, literature, writing, listening and speaking, and research in Illinois (Illinois State Board of Education, n.d.); and with the reading and writing standards of the National Council of Teachers of English and the International Reading Association (NCTE/IRA, 2009). They are consistent with Derek Bok's eight core competencies for college students (discussed in Austin, 2006). They are also consistent with the National Council for the Social Studies' Curriculum Guidelines for Multicultural Education (1991) as well as the criteria deemed important by the National Association for Multicultural Education for evaluating state curriculum standards themselves (National Association for Multicultural Education, 2001): The curriculum and pedagogy described in the following chapters reflect the values of inclusiveness, diverse perspectives, accommodating alternative epistemologies and social construction of knowledge, self-knowledge, and social justice.

Learning skills through multicultural content broadens the concept of developing skills in reading, research, writing, and communication in the English classroom. Reading texts from multiple cultures, writing well for a multicultural audience, and engaging in cross-cultural communication and community building strengthen students' skills in English language arts—skills in reading, writing, speaking, and listening—while also developing in students a broader ability to succeed in their multicultural world. Such an approach readies our students to take hold of contemporary societal challenges and to address those challenges with commensurate essential skills.

How Can Teachers Who Are Faced with the Push to Increase Students' Scores on Standardized Tests Use Multicultural Content to Attain These Scores?

In the early years of the 21st century I would ask us to return to the progressive thinking of John Dewey (1916/1966) in the early years of the 20th century. Dewey's framework for learning—starting with the student and the interests of the student, supporting his or her engagement in problem solving, and recognizing the importance of the social dimension of education—helps us understand the nature of engaged learning among our own students. Whether in learning to read, to write, to speak, or to listen, learning is tied to students' need to comprehend their world, to problem-solve, and to make meaning.

In this context, developing skills in reading and writing, speaking and listening cannot be the endpoint of learning, nor can a test be the goal of learning. Such skills become tools for interpretation, problem solving, and communication in society, and gaining these tools will best be facilitated within a shared community in the classroom. The chapters that follow describe students engaged in developing a wide range of skills in English language arts through a focus of study on multicultural texts and films.

Reading texts and screening films from across borders of race, culture, class, gender, and sexual orientation—a process explored throughout Chapters 2, 3, and 4—helps students develop an understanding of a broad array of American lives and issues; an understanding of multiple expressive forms; and skills in reading and visual comprehension, critical thinking, textual analysis, and vocabulary acquisition. Beyond texts and films grounded in multiple perspectives, the focus in this classroom expects students to be able to read and analyze background material and statistics relevant to the works of these artists; theories tied to social, psychological, economic, political, or cultural dynamics reflected in the literature and films; and scholarly essays that provide ways of thinking about lives and circumstances within the literature and films—all of which deepen and broaden students' interpretive skills, and all of which are tied to deepening their understanding of works of art and the workings of their society.

Discussions among students from multiple cultures about issues tied to race, class, gender, or sexual orientation, apparent throughout Chapters 2, 3, 4, and 6, provide students with experiences that foster skills in drawing on multiple perspectives; informed and logical thinking; clear, thoughtful, and effective articulation of ideas; and engaged listening. Such discussions also serve to strengthen cross-cultural awareness, sensitivity, communication, and problem solving.

Student-led presentations and discussions of scholarly and literary texts on issues of race, class, gender, or sexual orientation (Chapters 2, 3, 4, 6) strengthen students' skills in reading comprehension, vocabulary development, culling main points from complex texts, articulating points logically and clearly to others, facilitating the sharing of ideas within a group, and managing cross-cultural group dynamics.

Texts grounded in a broad range of perspectives, described throughout Chapters 2, 3, and 4, serve as models for students' own writing—exemplifying multiple ways of rendering one's own perspective and the perspectives of others and of thinking about, analyzing, or capturing one's world. As seen in Chapter 5, writing in journals primarily for the self as well as writing scripts, poetry, fiction, nonfiction, and digital nonfiction for an audience enable students to develop a fuller understanding of the nature and structure of multiple literary forms and skills in writing for self and others in a multicultural society.

Writing short and long analytical essays—seen in Chapters 2, 3, 4, and 5—deepens students' skills in close critical reading and film analysis; in research; in processing ideas from multiple types of texts and films across multiple cultures; in applying theories and perspectives grounded in texts and films from multiple cultures to real life; in constructing a sound, polished thesis, introduction, argument, and conclusion; and in employing a standard style of documentation.

A written exam—described in Chapters 2 and 3—helps students broaden skills in reading comprehension, comparing and contrasting theories and perspectives held by scholars and artists from multiple cultures on key issues, applying these theories and perspectives to new circumstances, and writing cogent discursive answers under the pressure of time.

As did Dewey long ago, each of us must ask ourselves about the students in our classrooms: Can they use what they are learning to successfully inhabit and interpret their world? In this classroom, students gain skills for effective participation in democratic life, such as reading for the pleasure of discovery and for a growing awareness and understanding of complex lives and issues emerging from multiple cultures. They gain skills for clear and informed thinking, speaking, and writing; engaged listening; developing community mindedness; seeing oneself as an agent of change; engaging in public dialogues through speaking, listening, or writing; and taking meaningful action. All these are skills that are consistent with broadly stated standards in English language arts for educating our students—and that move beyond them.

CONCLUSION

In this time and place, the more diverse the classroom and the more diverse the curriculum, the broader, the deeper, the more meaningful the learning experience is for us all. The multicultural classroom can be an exceptionally powerful arena that brings together the ideals of learning in a democratic society and the discipline to foster the growth of active citizens who read broadly, write effectively, listen closely, and speak out clearly for the greater good. These are the skills Americans seek in their young and the development for which they hold their schools and teachers responsible. In this classroom, they are achieved in the absence of standardized testing and through the power of education grounded in the perspectives of those from multiple cultures that constitute contemporary America. More broadly, schooling such as this offers a counterpoint to the pressures of racism, classism, sexism, heterosexism and homophobia, silence and invisibility that still surround these students. Such schooling says to all students that they are seen, recognized, and cherished for who they are, not only in hallways and classrooms but also in the focus of their studies. Our students deserve no less.

Exploring Race, Culture, and Gender
Through American Literature and Films:
Understanding Self and Others

Give them the best [literature] there is to engage them.

—Toni Morrison

I've had fun studying other cultures, but it's something about your own that particularly hits home. It's sort of like your curriculum. That makes me feel special and important.

—African American student

What struck me about "Shifting the Lens" was that it entirely depended on simply putting aside one's own perspective and considering another's.

—White student

PRELUDE

"Today," I said to the students, "we will explore contemporary Latino American writing and a work by Helena Maria Viramontes, 'The Moths.'"

It is an exquisite story, set in East L.A., of a young girl at odds with her strict father, her teasing sisters, and her family's Catholicism. But she is close to her grandmother, with whom she shares gardening, chayote vines, and cooking, and later with whom she will share the older woman's death. Instead of going to Mass one day, the young girl turns left to her abuelita's—because, she tells us, the church is cold, and empty, and lonely.

It is the girl who is caring for her dying grandmother, the girl who, that afternoon, prepares, unwittingly, her grandmother's last supper of Campbell's soup. It is the girl who discovers at sunset that her grandmother has stopped breathing. She takes out her grandmother's simple white towels, cradles her, lifts her into the bath, bathes her, and oversees her resurrection as she watches the gray moths of the soul soar upward and out of her body.

But in the quiet hush in this room after I finish reading the story come quickly emerging observations, the first ones from students who are often leaders in our discussions.

"This was so weird, she was with her naked grandmother in the bath."

22

Another student follows with, "We're so backward with sex."

I feel lost, adrift, as I watch this exquisite story drown under the ethnocentrism of the culture of dying and, for many of us, our disconnectedness from death, the body of death, and what it means to die at home, to touch those we love after they are gone, to cradle them.

A few others speak.

"This is just plain weird."

"Maybe it's the way we use language. We should use *nakedness*. She's naked; it's not about sex."

I wrestle with the journey we must take across the cultural borders so vividly drawn around each of the students in this multicultural classroom: how America is a multicultural nation and American literature is a multicultural literature, and how the customs of dying are tied to deep-seated cultural traditions. Many of the students in this classroom know and experience death only in a hospital, surrounded by the sound of machines. They may never touch or see the body and perhaps then only after it has been carefully prepared by a professional. For many of us, our family members no longer die at home, there to be touched and held past the moment of death.

I find this piece deeply spiritual and moving, every moment of the girl's closeness to her grandmother in life and in death and beyond: That she is only 14, the same age as my students. That I could not have had that strength at her age, that I found it only in snatches a few years ago, in my 50s, as I tried to soothe my ailing mother through bathing her forehead, to bathe away in part her fears.

And then one of the students brings us around. She reminds us that across the world, most people still do die at home and are held and carried into death by those who love them.

I say to these open-eyed gentle kids in front of me, "Yes, the practices that surround death are deeply embedded in our cultures."

In encountering this moment and in so many others, I tell the students: "If we can develop a multicultural perspective, we will develop a skill that will help us today and throughout our lives to see beyond our own borders, our own boundaries of the mind and expectations. To see the world through the eyes of others as they share it with us."

I'm not sure they understand that.

The last student to leave the room is a young Latina. She picks up her books. "Goodbye, Ms. D."

I am weeping inside—for the loneliness of death and dying, for the love of the child in this story, for my love of these children in front of me, for my sorrow at in some way failing this young Latina. If I had understood the moment better, I would have taken this group of kids where they needed to go before reading the story to them. I would have spared the young Latina her own loneliness at having a cultural tradition misunderstood, made alien, called weird. I would have done a better job. I would not have let her feel alone in this classroom filled with kids.

"Goodbye, Ms. D."

"Goodbye, Maria."

For another section of this same course that afternoon, I frame this gentle story for the students before reading it to them—in conversation with them about their own experiences with loss and how our customs in dealing with death are shaped within each of our cultures. This time, the moment I finish reading the story aloud, a young Latino, very close to his own grandparents and recently having lost one of his grandmothers, gently spontaneously applauds and then looks around the room sheepishly. This time, the students' responses—all of them—center around the closeness and the meaning of loss tied to their own grandparents. The story has spoken to all of these students across its cultural borders, and it has brought us closer together.

INTRODUCTION

All of the students in this classroom have grown up within one or more specific cultures that provide a context for their growth as young men and women. Their cultures have shaped perspectives, values, traditions, bodies of knowledge, personal and family histories, and expectations of who they will become as men and women. The journey we share in this course will allow each of these students, grounded in their own experiences and expectations tied to race, culture, and gender, to travel with scholars, writers, and filmmakers into a number of the cultures that define their nation. Through the works of these writers and artists, students will see lives and values that reflect or resemble their own as well as lives and values that acquaint them with wholly new perspectives. In the face of an increasingly diverse population, an increasing isolation of neighborhoods and schools by race and class, the persistence of racism and unequal opportunities by gender, little broad-spread meaningful integration of the multiple literary threads that constitute the literature of America in the teaching of American literature; and, too often, a reliance not on broad reading itself to create an educated populace, but on the relentless hammer of timed testing, there is a crucial need for our students to read America.

READING FOR REAL, READING AMERICA

Students enter our schools and our classrooms full of questions. As Dewey (1916/1966) reminds us, that curiosity, the need to know, fuels the most passionate and engaged learning. What do these students wonder about? All of these students are on a journey of discovery, and their search for identity often brings together aspects of race, culture, and gender. At the center of their questions are often two primary sets of questions. One is about race or culture: Who am I? Who are you? What does it mean to be White, to be a person of color, to be biracial, to be a cross-cultural adoptee? And one is about gender: What does it mean to be a man or a woman? And what does it mean to be a man or a woman in a particular culture? Their sense of self is often twofold: I am a woman and I am a Chicana. I am a man and I am Jewish. Their senses of their racial, cultural, and gender identities are often entwined.

They also want to know how to successfully navigate the multicultural society that surrounds them. They want to know why we still have problems with segregation and racism. They want to know about language—about how to refer to those in other cultures. They have questions about personal choices that involve cross-cultural dynamics. And they have questions, emerging from their cultural moorings, about gender definitions, expectations, and roles. They are also attempting to untangle the differences between what's real and what are the powerful stereotypes that have surrounded them growing up—about those in their own culture and in other cultures and about men or women.

The best writers across the United States can offer these students answers to many of their questions. Over the next months in this course, we will journey across America listening to scholars, writers, and filmmakers on individual, family, and societal circumstances that reflect issues of race, culture, and gender, and the factors that support or restrict lives, bring us together or push us apart (Appendix B).

What happens when we steep students in a less familiar, broad spectrum of American scholars, writers, and artists; when we read across the borders of race, culture, and gender and look together at the issues these scholars, writers, and filmmakers want us to think about? What happens when we really read America? What does this look like? What are the effects on individuals and the group? Why is it important to do this?

Come, join us as we read America.

Starting Points: Thoughts on Pedagogy

All of the works in this course have a number of elements in common. They all speak to one aspect or another of these students' world. They represent a broad range of perspectives from men and women across the multiple cultures that make up American life. They focus on young lives. Overwhelmingly, these scholars and artists come from the culture that is the focus of their work. And reading and connecting with these works often require border crossings—journeys that are not always automatic or easy or clear for students.

Because this type of study expects students to shift perspectives constantly, providing guidelines for discussions and providing background and context for each writer and work is crucial. At the beginning of the course, I explain to students that we will be viewing our world from many different perspectives. All of the issues these works raise and that we will examine are complex and generate multiple points of view; this is what makes them compelling and complicated, and, at times, difficult to discuss. All of us need to feel we can be honest, but it is crucial that we also be sensitive to the ways in which our ideas and our words, our speaking, listening, or actions can affect our classmates. Respectful dialogues are crucial in this type of learning. Because of the border crossings that will be necessary for all of these students, it is also crucial to provide them with background on each segment of the course; each scholar, writer, or filmmaker; and each work itself. Students need to be able to make cognitive and affective leaps to enter many of these pieces. Establishing a background and context enables them to begin that process. It also establishes a respectful framework for the writer and his or her world and perspective. Establishing a context for the work helps students begin the movement into a less familiar perspective and thus minimizes the disorientation that may lead to spontaneous, uniformed observations that can easily derail a conversation or strain group cohesiveness. Context for scholar, artist, and work can begin to loosen the rigidity of culture-bound knowledge, expectations, and assumptions.

Not establishing such a context can damage students' experience of a work and leave the group strained or fractured. I learned this in a series of painful moments years ago in a course for freshmen. The class was predominantly White, and we were studying the work of Latina writer Helena Maria Viramontes (1995b). The memory of that moment, described in the Prelude to this chapter, haunts me still.

Another crucial aspect of this type of teaching is respecting the psychological function and power of resistance. As students cross borders, they are being asked to leave a comfortable and familiar perspective. Asking any students to move too far too quickly from the familiar and the comfortable sets off a protective resistance. While that resistance reestablishes a sense of personal equilibrium, it can also close off important moments of learning. I try to be cognizant of the expectations and effects of this type of learning: that some students will need to dramatically shift their paradigms of thinking—paradigms that may have been taught and encouraged throughout their childhoods. Some of them are also being asked to examine perspectives and issues—and participate in a process—that asks them to share or yield power. Thus, it is important that the journey we take—for all students—be a pleasurable one in many ways, that it please and reward individuals and the group for their curiosity, their thoughtfulness, and respect. And so I make sure that for every work, I help the students begin their movement from one or more perspectives to another—through enabling them to first meet the writers, artists, and their worlds and the issues that are significant to them. This helps the students begin to take the steps across the border between worlds more gradually. If we can reside in the region of learning that taps students' natural and broad-based curiosity about their world and their goodwill, we can cover much ground, inviting them into a wide range of perspectives and avoiding a level of resistance that makes learning impossible.

Preparation

To prepare for our journey, we read the works of several scholars who give us metaphors and theories for thinking about the ways in which race, culture, and gender operate in our lives. For Arturo Madrid (2007), that metaphor is a building. Some are invited in the front door, some aren't; for those excluded, their job is to get in through any opening they can. For Marilyn Frye (2007), with special attention to the lives of women, it's a birdcage. Oppression works as do the bars on the cage—look at one and there is no entrapment, stand back and you understand the cage that entraps. For Ronald Takaki (2007), it's "a different mirror" necessary for Americans to alter their notion of who an American is; for Cherríe Moraga (2007), it's the color of our skin; and for June Jordan (1995), it's the unpredictable connections that bring us together—whether those connections occur through a shared culture, color, gender, class, or need. Beginning in this segment and throughout the course, individual students are asked to frame for the group the main ideas they feel are germane to a given essay and to lead the discussion of key points and passages (Appendix B). It's Frye's essay that sets off the students' earliest spirited debate. Her analogy of the birdcage for oppression is fleshed out by young women in the group focusing on women's restricted movement in their daily lives. Her ideas immediately have resonance for these big-city students who know the discrepancies between the freedom of movement accorded young men on city streets and the need for caution for young women. But several young Black men remind us that they don't feel free at all on these city streets infamous for racial profiling.

We turn next to the documentary film *School Colors* (Andrews, 1994) and nestle into a year with the diverse senior class of Berkeley High School in Berkeley, California. My students see students their own age wrestle with the same challenges they face in a multiracial society: Is tracking necessary to facilitate better learning for all students or a betrayal of students of color and poor students based on race and class? Who should have power—and in what language—on the student newspaper? Why have an African American Studies Department? Students feel passionate about many moments in the film, such as a young Chicana being rejected for dating a White boy and the notion of separate graduations for students in separate cultures.

For one young White student in our classroom the film triggered multi-faceted thinking about race and class in American public schools—and the need to ensure equality of access for all students. An excerpt captures some of her thinking: "One of the biggest flaws in the American education system is the way it is intrinsically linked to economics. Equality in education must begin as soon as school begins. When children start learning out of a desire to learn, and they are not forced into a bad system only because their parents were in it, then equality can truly begin."

For a young Asian student living in the United States, the film was much more personal, allowing her to feel less alone: "This week we've been watching *School Colors* in our class. Every time when we go into a scene with the Chinese student Arthur, my heart races. Then he said it! He feels awkward inviting his American friends to his house. Some of my classmates gave out signs of pity. But I completely understood him. No, I don't want to be thought of as more of something odd, strange, or weird. I refuse to invite classmates over."

These texts, metaphors, and film simultaneously give us a language to talk about issues of race, culture, and gender, and, in our responses to them, initiate our own cross-cultural dialogues about these issues. They also initiate the students' first analytical writing in the course as they select one of several options and craft a two-page analytical essay making connections among concepts or metaphors from the scholarly essays, moments or issues in *School Colors*, and moments or issues within their own school (Appendix B).

For the remainder of our time together, we will move across America, visiting with scholars, writers, and filmmakers, as well as men, women, and children from diverse cultures, all of whom will offer us additional perspectives for looking out on issues tied to race and culture—and, within those contexts, gender. Our exploration of issues of gender within the context of race and culture reflects the findings of the authors of *Race, Gender, and Work*: "We do not believe that race-ethnicity, gender, or class can be correctly understood isolated from one another, for they have been constructed and experienced simultaneously" (Amott & Matthaei, 1996, p. 5).

A JOURNEY ACROSS AMERICA

Latino American Perspectives

Our segment on Latino lives opens with screening a *Frontline* documentary, *Children of the Harvest* (Court & Arango, 1998), as background for students reading, outside of class, Tomas Rivera's (1992) classic novella about migrant lives and labor, *And the Earth Did Not Devour Him*. These city students are immediately drawn into the film as the camera pans across open fields or citrus groves, revealing Latino children of all ages filling tin pails with fruits or vegetables alongside their parents. We see the children working long hours, sleeping several to a bed in temporary housing, and playing gentle games in the evenings. My students see children much younger than they picking cucumbers and packing blueberries as they nod toward sleep at the end of a long day of standing. One White farmer explains it's good for kids to work with their parents.

The next day students bring in their responses to both the film and Rivera's novella. Initially they are a bit puzzled by scenes in the novella of lives so removed from their own, but as they begin to fill the chalkboard with the images that Rivera's young narrator gives us as he recalls a year on the migrant cycle, they begin to see in front of them the pieces of a young life emerge: open-air trucks that break down, mothers lost in dime stores, barbers who refuse to cut the young boy's hair, heat strokes, and wondering why bad things happen to good people, with the young narrator eventually adding it all up and realizing that he is not lost, but found—in the memories of his own community. We also talk about the exquisite design of the work—that its language, multiple voices, and fragmentary stories mirror aspects of the migrant experience itself. After looking at both works, my students are full of questions: Should the father of the large family in the film be able to let his children help the family earn an income? Or should the government step in and prevent it? Why do these conditions exist in farm labor? And are those conditions tied to the fact that the workers are Latinos? In both film and novella, these students are taken into what feels like a faraway world, but they also realize that that world is as close as their neighborhood market and the fresh food on their table. It's a lot for these kids to piece together: about families and culture; cross-cultural dynamics involving identity, power, and survival; love and closeness and poverty; farm labor; exploitation; and government regulations—or their failure. For one young African American woman in class, the images of migrants come very close to home and are a reminder of what her own family has accomplished: "Reading *And the Earth Did Not Devour Him* made me think about the stories that my grandmother and great-grandmother tell me about their time spent picking cotton. I am proud of everything that these leading ladies did. My grandmother is a true inspiration to me, because she went from picking cotton to being a nurse. Through her actions I am reminded that anything is possible and that education is the key to opening the door of possibility."

Our next readings take us into the work of writers Judith Ortiz Cofer and Helena Maria Viramontes. Ortiz Cofer (2007) explores in a personal essay the continuing power of stereotypes in a life. And fiction writer Helena Maria Viramontes (1995a) gives us portraits of struggling neighborhood lives and immigrant terrors in East L.A. in "The Cariboo Café."

Last, we meet an ebullient upscale family consisting of a widowed father and his three grown daughters living the American Dream in L.A. in Maria Ripoll's film *Tortilla Soup* (2004). Watching students watch this film is instructive in itself: Many are entranced—delighted—with every vivid scene; others are puzzled: "What is this, a chic flick?" "Why are we watching this?" What becomes clear in follow-up discussions is that many of these students, having been reared in a society so replete with negative media stereotypes of Latinos, are completely disoriented by the daily lives of this elegant, loving, and enviable Latino family. The film debunks in every way encircling familiar stereotypes of Latinos. For two young women of color the power of the film is clear: "Why aren't there more films like this shown, Ms. D.?" "It's so important for kids of color to see themselves in successful positions."

Because students always want to know where stereotypes come from, as we move through the course, we examine a series of commentaries on stereotypes tied to each group we study. In this segment we look at two handouts on the nature and power of Latino stereotypes (Garcia Berumen, 1996; "Unlearning," 2002), as well as theories and research on the origins of prejudice (Stephan, 1999). In "The Chicano/Hispanic Image in American Films," teacher and film follower Garcia Berumen (1996) cautions us that stereotypes in American media are not benign and have the power to derail the schooling of young Latinos, as overpowering negative images affect their sense of self and relation to their first language. "Unlearning Chicano, Latino, and Puerto Rican Stereotypes" (2002) reflects the fact that administrators at one university feel the effect of stereotypes can have such a negative impact on university life that they give new students this handout to "unlearn them." During our last class looking at Latino issues, students reexamine the images of Latinos in the works of Rivera, Court and Arango, Viramontes, Ortiz Cofer, and Ripoll in the context of these theories about stereotypes and prejudice. One group of students wonders if the decision to use the handout at the university in fact teaches stereotypes rather than lessens them. Looking up from the pages spread out in front of her, one young Latina says quietly: "What we see is that there is

no resemblance between the stereotypes and these individuals. The stereotypes show no grief, no reality."

What do the students take from these varied images? For many, the
most persistent images are those of close, loving, or hardworking families.
Others, however, observe that in all of these works except *Tortilla Soup*, a
romantic comedy, writers are concerned with the power of multiple factors
to constrict in one way or another the potential of these individuals as men
or as women.

After this segment of the course, students write their second short analytical paper, bringing together a series of perspectives on socioeconomic
class from an opening segment of the course and their study of Latino lives
and issues. Students may opt to examine the lives of Latino characters
through the lens of factors that support or inhibit upward mobility or the
relationship between Latino stereotypes and the real lives of Latinos; com-
pare and contrast a scholarly essay and a personal essay on the workings
of socioeconomic class in individual lives; or, similar to a personal essay by
Richard Rodriguez, write their own personal essay about "coming to class
consciousness" (Appendix B).

African American Lives and Communities

The next week, we turn to African American lives and issues. In class, Spike
Lee (2001) shows us the power of those in power in multiple industries to
promulgate inaccurate and damaging images of a people for decade after
decade in his film *Bamboozled*. Outside of class students read Toni Morrison's (1973) novel *Sula*, where we meet men, women, and children in the
metaphorical "Bottom," a poor but thriving Black community in Ohio.

Lee's complex and layered satire leaves no one untouched in his exploration of those whose work has reduced the dignity of Black life to cari-
cature in metal coin banks, cartoons, postcards, or on film, television, or
stage. Some students are thrown by the film's psychological complexity: Was
I supposed to laugh? Why did I feel so uncomfortable? Others are almost
overwhelmed by the tragedy at its core. One young Black woman wrote,
"At the end of *Bamboozled*, I cried for the grief of my people." For one Jewish student, Lee's work in *Bamboozled* further confirmed one truth about
American media: "The media is an instrument of mainstream society, and
by selectively choosing the manner in which Blacks are portrayed, clearly
preferring buffoonery to intelligence and success, is complicit in shaping
distorted views of Blacks that so many accept as truth."

Sula is an equally complex work of art for these students. In this tour
de force, Morrison probes the strength, vitality, and vulnerability of African
American men and women, and the power of women's friendships. Through

unforgettable characters—Nel; Sula; Plum; the Deweys; or poor, one-legged Eva Peace, overseeing a sprawling household from her perch on a child's wagon—Morrison opens up the impact of war, unequal power across races, limited possibilities for individual fulfillment for adults or children, as well as the steadfast and sustaining strength of close relationships and the community itself. She makes clear the factors that have prevented African American men from having satisfying work of their own during the best years of their lives—and the impact of that on their own lives, their families, and their community, generation after generation. Both Nel, a consummately warm and caring wife and mother, and her closest friend Sula, fiercely free, bold, and independent, remain strong, smart, and loving Black women who hold families and communities together. But their fates remind us of the price some of these strong women pay. Nel's husband, after a brief affair with Sula, leaves Nel to face the rest of her life alone; Sula's bold independence alienates most of those around her, her brief display of dependency frightens off the one man she has grown close to, and she dies alone.

For some White students, because Morrison works obliquely in *Sula*, initially there is a sense of confusion: "Why did we read this?" It's not until our discussion unveils the real workings of each of these characters that the novel becomes a metaphor for the history of one Black American community from slavery through the civil rights movement to the eventual gentrification and destruction of the neighborhood and the continued restrictions placed on the lives of Black men, women, and children by forces seen and unseen. This young Black woman's observation captured the power of the work for many of the students: "I could not get enough of *Sula*. Even though people such as Shadrack would try and protest injustices, they would soon die, which means that no matter what Blacks try to do to make things balanced between the two races, something always happens to tear down that dream."

The next day, students meet the work of scholars Cornel West (2004) on hip-hop and Orlando Patterson (2006) on the challenges facing some young Black men in American cities. Film clips take us onto the streets of L.A. and the lure of gangs for young men—and women—with few resources (Bendau, 1994), as well as into the work of Tommy the Clown as he provides an alternative to gangs in a form of competitive dancing called "clowning" in the film *Rize* (LaChapelle, 2005). West's words speak directly to what one young bicultural musician in the class has seen around him: that for Black musicians, a growing sense of "Black nihilism" has come directly from feeling valued neither by their society nor by themselves. And some of these film images of gang members describing their needs come very close to home for one young Latina, who tells us they describe exactly what she has seen in her previous neighborhood.

On our last day on African American writers and artists, student discussion leaders open up essays by Eduardo Bonilla-Silva (2007) on "racism without racists," a new and perhaps more insidious form of racism, and the option of Whites to choose whether or not to identify themselves by their ethnicities—an option, according to author Mary Waters (2007), not available to people of color.

We end this focus with a series of images by young Black artists on YouTube: Chris Rock gives us an only partly comic look at racial profiling in *How Not to Get Your Ass Kicked by the Police* (n.d.), and Daniel Beaty (2003) in *Def Poetry Jam* shares his poem "Duality Duel: The Nigger and the Nerd," about one young man's inner conflict in living with a dual identity. In the midst of Beaty's performance piece on the screen in front of our darkened classroom, one young Black student, poised between two worlds in her own life, spontaneously stands up and calls out, "Yes, yes! That's me, that's what it's like!" One young Chinese student later describes in a journal entry the ways in which the same piece has spoken to her: The young Black student's public affirmation of the piece has told her that she is not alone. In the midst of each of these students confronting their own challenges of assimilation, and prompted by a moment of Black performance art, a friendship begins. In our last work, filmmaker Byron Hurt (2008), in *Barack & Curtis: Manhood, Power & Respect/Examining Black Masculinity*, suggests that Barack and Michelle Obama have ushered in a new era for Black men and women. Throughout this segment, as students assemble their own thoughts, their observations are often as accurate—and as haunting in their accuracy—as those of many of these artists and scholars.

Asian Americans: Strangers at Home

Our exploration of Asian American lives and issues begins with Frank Chin's (1991) novella *Donald Duk*, about young Donald Duk, an 11-year-old Chinese American student living with his thriving family in San Francisco's Chinatown and attending, in his words, a "snooty White private school." Initially teased in his own neighborhood and at school about his name, and embarrassed about his life in Chinatown, Donald begins a journey of discovery that results in his embracing the strength of his Chinese history and culture, correcting erroneous information at school, and finding a comfortable sense of self moving daily among two cultures. The novella is wonderful for so many reasons—addressing in one story the feelings of many students of color attending predominantly White schools or any students juggling life in more than one cultural context and the culturally imbalanced teaching of American history, as well as questions of identity, the nature of truth, and how we know what we know. It is a complex little novel moving the reader in and out of dreams and reality for young Donald, but it results in wide-ranging discussions about multiple issues in the world of these students. The only weakness of the novel is Chin's depiction of women, as he has admittedly been interested with reconstructing the image of the Asian American male; this, too, is something we explore in our discussions.

At the beginning of this segment, we also spend one day in a workshop on racial identity development theory and models. The theory and models enable students to have a broader understanding of young Donald Duk's struggle with his identity and provide ways of thinking about their own emerging identities. Students are given a handout containing a brief explanation of the theory of racial identity development and several different racial identity development models (Ponterotto, Casas, Suzuki, & Alexander, 1995; Poston, 1990; Tatum, 1992). In a society that has decided "race matters," everyone will develop a racial identity, but because of the history of American race relations, that process will differ for Whites, individuals of color, and biracial individuals. This workshop always elicits a range of strong responses. Both White students and students of color are intrigued with the notion of a racial identity development process and often find the models helpful in understanding observations they have made about themselves and others. Biracial students have said out loud, "I've experienced every step in this process."

Students across multiple cultures identify with many of the challenges facing young Donald. Like Donald, many of these students are students of color in a predominantly White school; they, too, have wanted more emphasis on their own cultures in the pages of their learning. And all of the students in this room are engaged in discoveries about identity. Students also connect with Donald because he shows them the power of racism to distort one's sense of self, the value of questioning inherited information, and the value of research to learn the facts about the histories of cultures not frequently taught in American schools or taught through the lens of the dominant White culture. For one Asian American student, one of the most important perspectives Frank Chin provided was how education can affect minority students in America: "Education in America has the potential to be so great, yet on many processes it fails to deliver. Being Chinese is something to be ashamed of in America, and I think school has a large part in making Donald hate his culture." Donald's story spoke equally strongly to a Black student who remembered, at one point as a young boy in this predominantly White school, rejecting both his name and "his people." In time, he noted, he, too, like Donald, came to stick up for himself and for Blacks. One White student wrote that seeing San Francisco's Chinatown through Donald's family and experiences had completely changed the way he now experiences Chinatown in Chicago.

As students read Chin's novella outside of class, in class we turn to a scholarly essay by Yen Le Espiritu (2007) on the origin, nature, and intended effects, historically, of stereotypes of Asian American men and women. The reading provides a historical and cultural context for the works that follow. Comedian Margaret Cho in videos on YouTube has us both bent over in laughter and emerging with a sobering understanding of the reality of stereotypes as she mirrors an airline attendant's reservations in serving Asian chicken salad to an Asian American passenger (Cho, *Margaret Cho—Korea/Asian Chicken Salad*, n.d.) or as she mocks her reception as an Asian American by her boyfriend's White parents (Cho, *Margaret Cho Talks About Race*, n.d.). We spend time with Maya Lin and her "strong clear vision" in a documentary film of the young designer who, as a student at Yale, was awarded the opportunity to design the Vietnam War Memorial and then faced bitter opposition to the award going to an Asian American woman (Mock, 2003). Lastly, we screen the documentary *The Cats of Mirikitani* (Hattendorf, 2008), tracing the lifelong effects of the internment of Japanese Americans during World War II on one individual, Jimmy Mirikitani, a gentle and reflective Japanese American artist living on the streets of New York City during the attacks on the World Trade Center, still having been unable to reestablish a viable economic base or a sense of trust in his own country.

For my students, all of these men's and women's lives offer a dramatic contrast to the sinister, sexualized, or submissive stereotypes of Asian American men or women fostered for decades in this country (Espiritu, 2007). And the feminist art of Cho relentlessly challenges these images. The lives in these works also reveal the strength of individual men and women—and children—in the face of racism, whether within schools, the populace, or the government.

At the end of this section, students are asked to gather their thoughts in a midterm exam. Although the exam provides students with a choice among questions, the experience requires them to pull together multiple perspectives on a wide range of issues and to have a basic grasp of each scholar's, writer's, or filmmaker's vision (Appendix B).

Jewish Americans: The Holocaust and Beyond

Our examination of issues emerging from Jewish lives in America moves from literature and art tied to the Holocaust to fiction writers and scholars focusing on contemporary issues. We begin with the focus "Who can tell our histories and how?: Making art about traumatic cultural history" through screening the film version of William Styron's controversial novel *Sophie's Choice* (Pakula, 1998), about two young men and a young woman in NYC, each coming to terms with the impact of history. We also read Art

Spiegelman's (1991) controversial, award-winning "comic book" *Maus II*, about the impact of the Holocaust on his own family. Students are asked to ponder, respectively, (1) the difference between the insider and the outsider in telling our stories and the impact of that perspective (Styron is not Jewish, and Sophie is not Jewish but Polish Catholic) and (2) the use of the graphic novel and animal characters for exploring this period in history.

For the students, each work is intriguing and each work disturbs. For one Jewish student, watching *Sophie's Choice* is less overwhelming than she feared, because it focuses on one mother rather than on massive losses in the camps. For others, it's a devastatingly sad film that captures the long-term effects of such sweeping trauma on diverse lives. For a young Polish American woman, the experience proves very personal: "Watching *Sophie's Choice* this week has put what my great-grandfather went through into perspective. My great-grandfather was a survivor and died one year ago. I remember as a child my great-grandfather telling me what he had gone through. He had this uniform from jail hanging on the wall to constantly remember all of those who were noble but were not as fortunate to survive as he."

Reading *Maus II* has surprised some students: The images of animals have made the reality of the Holocaust even scarier for some; for others, they have provided a necessary distance to approach this period. For one young Asian student, the graphic novel results in no less than an epiphany about history: "Everything is inseparable from history. History really makes us who we are, in terms of our personality, identity, behavior, interactions with everyone around us; and gives us our frame of reference. The effects of history are truly astounding and perplexing." She ends up exploring this idea further—across multiple cultures and lives—in her final paper for the course.

We move to post-Holocaust literature with Bernard Malamud's (1983) "The Jewbird," an allegorical tale of the displaced wandering Jew looking for a home in America and being rebuffed by a comfortably assimilating Jewish family; and from there to Joanna Spiro's (1996) contemporary meditation on Jewish American identity among the young, "Three Thousand Years of Your History, Take One Year for Yourself." We end this study with two scholarly essays on aspects of Jewish identity: "From 'Kike' to 'JAP': How Misogyny, Anti-Semitism, and Racism Construct the 'Jewish American Princess'" (Beck, 1995) and "What White Supremacists Taught a Jewish Scholar About Identity" (Ferber, 2007).

The day we discuss the scholarly essays, a young Jewish woman, an alumna of our school and this course, joins us; she takes part in the discussion of both essays and shares with these high school seniors a glimpse back into social dynamics across cultures on her college campus. The essay "From

'Kike' to 'JAP'" triggers a particularly animated discussion as students share disparate understandings not only of the term but of its power in their lives. As students talk over these works, it's clear that many of them have thought about, puzzled over, and been affected by the term *Jewish American princess* and that the anti-Semitism among Jews that troubles Malamud is not only familiar to these Jewish students but is parallel to racism among individuals within the same culture in other cultures. It is also clear that many of these students have a spiritual home in another country—similar to Rachel's notion of Israel in Spiro's short story. With these essays and our guest speaker's perspectives fresh in their thinking, many of the students wonder what cross-cultural dynamics they will encounter as they themselves move onto college campuses the next year.

Students also see in these works multiple ways in which aspects of culture figure in the development of a sense of self and sense of fulfillment for men and women. Sweeping violence tied to her cultural identity and her gender during the Holocaust decimates Sophie's life as a woman after World War II. The trauma and losses of the Holocaust leave Spiegelman tormented with guilt, searching for a meaning to his family's life and his own life, no matter his success as writer and artist. Beck's essay, too, provides a powerful glimpse into the relationship between culture and gender. In dissecting the term *Jewish American princess* and looking at "how misogyny, anti-Semitism, and racism" created the epithet, the author probes origins and elements of the stereotype, its relation to Jewish fathers and mothers, and its ongoing effects on Jewish women. In each of the works explored here, for Nathan in *Sophie's Choice*, for writer-artist Art Spiegelman, and for scholars Ferber and Beck, as well as for Spiro's young character Rachel, development and expression of their lives as men or women is intimately linked with their exploration of the meaning of Jewish identity, Judaism, Israel, or anti-Semitism in their lives; or, for Sophie, with her identity as a Polish woman.

After this segment, students write their third short analytical paper, focusing on issues explored in this section and in a segment of the course on gay, lesbian, bisexual, and transgender lives and issues. Grounded in our readings and films, students can explore the relationship of Jewish identity to place, relationships, strategies for coping with anti-Semitism, or aspects of gender roles (Appendix B).

Biracial, Multiethnic Lives: Identity, Place, and Belonging

If all students enter this room with questions about who they are as individuals and as young men or young women, those questions may be broadened if the students are biracial or multiethnic. And if students of color often find few representations of themselves and their experiences in the focal points and readings in their courses, this is even more so for biracial or multiethnic students—despite the rapidly growing population of individuals who identify as such. Both biracial and multiethnic students and students who identify with a single culture, however, are drawn to these stories and films about individuals, couples, and families who bring together multiple cultures.

Our exploration of biracial, multiethnic lives opens with a review of the history of the status of biracial relationships in this country, as well as statistics and issues relevant to contemporary biracial and multiethnic lives (Hamako, 2005). For students with experience in biracial relationships, the history and context of antimiscegenation laws opens one door into more understanding about the stares and unkindness they sometimes encounter, even in as large and diverse a city as Chicago. We screen part of the documentary film *An American Love Story* (Fox, 1999), meeting a close and loving biracial family in New York City as their oldest daughter, Cicily, leaves for Colgate University. Outside of class, students select three essays to read in *Half and Half: Writers on Gowing Up Biracial and Bicultural* (O'Hearn, 1998), a rich collection of personal essays about lives lived across multiple cultures or continents. As students explore these essays, they meet biracial or multiethnic individuals, couples, and families, as well as individuals whose histories include one or more transcontinental moves. All of these writers share with us aspects of their discoveries about identity, place, and belonging. This focus ends with screening the feature film *Mississippi Masala* (Nair, 2003), in which Indian-born filmmaker Mira Nair traces the intersecting lives of a young Asian Indian woman who has recently fled from Uganda to the American South and a young African American man living and working in small-town Mississippi.

For many of the biracial or multiethnic individuals in these essays and films, as for many of the students in this room, the multifaceted nature of their cultural identities leads them to questions about expectations placed upon them as young men and women. Cicily's embrace of both Black and White aspects of her identity creates tensions for her with some of the young Black men and some of the young White men at Colgate. It is within a predominantly White sorority—among women—that she finds the comfort of belonging. The young Asian Indian woman and young southern American Black man in *Mississippi Masala* are caught within the diverging expectations of those close to them in their different cultures of origin as they attempt to build a loving relationship in Mississippi. For my students, Meena's and Demetrius's challenges capture some of their own families' issues tied to bringing together multiple cultures and, for some, the profound and wide-ranging challenges of immigration; but the film also draws forward my students' appreciation for the generally accepting environment they experience within a large diverse city and a progressive school.

My own bicultural students readily connect with many aspects of the lives of the bicultural individuals and families in these stories, and all of the students begin to develop an understanding of some of the challenges—as well as an appreciation for the broad and varied experiences and perspectives—reflected in the lives of parents, children, individuals, and couples who bring together multiple cultures. One young bicultural woman in the course explained simply, "I really connected to the biracial readings. I saw myself." Another explained how she had realized that her biracial identity allowed her to move comfortably in both Black and White worlds. A number of Jewish students found the essays in *Half and Half* particularly compelling, as the life stories reflected there gave them ways to understand their own lives, straddling their Jewish identity and culture at home and in their synagogue and the cultural values of the larger society, or their lives in families whose mothers and fathers embrace different religions. Some produced unusually probing and thoughtful meditations on contemporary Jewish identity in their final papers as a result. One young Black man, who had recently immigrated to the United States in stages from across several continents, embraced every moment of *Mississippi Masala*: "Yes," he said, "this film captured how hard it is in so many ways."

Arab Americans: Building Lives in a Tumultuous Time

Our last visit is with Arab American or Muslim individuals, couples, and families. Again, we open with handouts of facts and statistics, about Arabs living in the United States and about issues Arabs in the United States have faced since the attacks on the World Trade Center (ADC, "The Arab-American Community," n.d.; ADC, "Facts About Islam," n.d.; Al-Qatami, 2004). Most of my students have not known many Arab Americans, and they are stunned to learn that most Arab Americans are Christian and that their levels of achievement in education and their earnings are very high. What they are less surprised by are the pervasive negative images of Arabs and Muslims in American films captured in an award-winning, 9-minute film called *Planet of the Arabs* (Salloum, 2005), saturated with inaccurate images of Arabs in desert settings and cast as terrorists. Readings in *Dinarzad's Children: An Anthology of Contemporary Arab American Fiction* (Kaldas & Mattawa, 2004), the first collection of Arab American short fiction, introduces students to the needs and challenges of Arab Americans creating lives here, having fled conflicts throughout the Middle East, and trying to reach across cultural barriers to build lives and friendships in a new country. The documentary film *Brothers and Others* (Rossier, 2004) takes us to the New York City area and the struggles of Arabs, Muslims, and South Asians to maintain relationships, jobs, family lives, the traditional roles for men and women, and small businesses in the wake of the events of September 11, 2001. Lastly, in the essay "Chappals and Gym Shorts: An Indian Muslim Woman in the Land of Oz" (Sayeed, 2007), we meet a young Indian Muslim woman on a university campus in Kansas attempting to integrate the expectations of her traditional family—including an arranged marriage—with her own leanings toward the freedom, customs, and practices of independent women in the United States.

In this time and place, some of these students are uncertain about the focus on Arab American lives, but they approach it with openness and curiosity. One White student wrote in his journal at the beginning of this section of the course:

> Coming into the Arab-American portion of his class, I have no idea what to expect. Perhaps this is because Arab Americans are not a "mainstream minority," if there can be such a thing. Basically the only time you hear about Arab Americans is in the context of 9/11. I think that is why there are so many stereotypes of Arab Americans! We only get a narrow view of them. For example, when we learned that the majority of Arab Americans were Christian, it blew me away, and I consider myself fairly knowledgeable about different races and ethnicities in America. Hopefully this section will be able to break down more of my previous stereotypes.

For some, their sense of Jewish identity and history complicates their coming to this focal point. As one Jewish student wrote:

> I remarked in class today that it's very hard for me to be sympathetic towards Arab-American causes because I am Jewish, and most Muslim countries abhor Jews and are bent on the destruction of Israel. I felt that Muslims hate Jews and Jews hate Muslims. (I didn't know where this hatred came from—maybe it's deep history.) Because of this, I feel wary and skeptical of Arabs. However I've noticed something strange in my thinking. I may hate Muslims in Middle East theocracies, but I am improperly blurring the lines between Middle East Muslims and Arab Americans. As our handout said, the majority of Arabs in this country are Christian. How can I have animosity towards Arab Americans because of my dislike of Islam when most

Arab Americans aren't Muslim? The answer is I can't. I need to think about this issue more.

Arab American students, too, may come to this focus with mixed feelings. On the one hand, there is a tremendous sense of satisfaction in seeing this focus, these writers, and these films included in this course and the opportunity for classmates to learn more about their culture. On the other hand, they know that some of their classmates have little real familiarity with Arab Americans and that some are uneasy with this focus. And in fact, some Arab American students have tended to tuck aside their identity to make life easier for themselves.

Conversations throughout this segment are full of questions, sometimes tense, often generous, as we tentatively explore a culture unfamiliar to so many of these students. One young bicultural Arab American explained her initial feelings—and her hopes:

> Our first day discussing Arab Americans was so hard for me. I've never really met another Arab outside of my family so I often feel alone. I felt like when we were talking about Arabs and the stereotypes against them, that no one took it as seriously as me. At one point I felt myself getting really anxious and I thought that I was going to cry. It was basically because I felt like no one understood what it felt like to be an Arab in today's society. I just hope that after this unit, people will start to understand us a little bit better.

What these students' observations mean is that their starting points for coming together in this segment of our study are farther apart than they have been when we have focused on cultures and lives more familiar to them; their uncertainties, prejudices, and vulnerabilities are a bit more pronounced. We have farther to go to be able to come together as we share this focus.

Gradually, however, all of the students begin to absorb multiple new perspectives and the conversations become more informed and more relaxed. By the time we discuss the stories in *Dinarzad's Children*, the students are readily making cross-cultural leaps: A story on a strained love affair between an Egyptian American woman and Jewish American man invites comparisons with the students' own cross-cultural relationships and how complex they can sometimes be. One young Jewish student's comment reflected the essence of many of the students' observations in response to the documentary film *Brothers and Others*: "I was shocked about the documentary because I did not know to what extent the government was intruding in on the lives of both citizens and immigrants." And Sayeed's essay prompts a broad and animated discussion about the challenges Sayeed herself faces trying to be who she is in the context of two cultures and two radically different sets of expectations—as an Indian Muslim living in America and as a woman—something many of these young women, coming from diverse cultures and testing their roles as women, can relate to. One young Latina later wrote, "From Sayeed, we learned a great deal about how culture and gender can affect the life of an individual." The films and readings have taken students into new perspectives.

One year, the author of the short story "Shakespeare in the Gaza Strip" (Kayyal, 2004)—about the misguided intentions of an American teacher abroad—joins us for a discussion of the story. She is married, with two daughters; she lives, teaches, and writes in a suburb of Chicago. As she enters the room, she carries an armload of handmade bookmarks. On each she has outlined in gold ink the figure of a dove; the dove's eye a bright blue gem affixed to the paper, a branch in his beak. The bookmarks are gifts she has made and brought to each of the students. The dove represents peace, she says to the students, and gift-giving is a tradition in her culture. She is young and warm and vivacious. She speaks of her family, her daughters, her daughters living in two worlds as they travel back and forth between the United States and Palestine, and the fact that her daughters' friends can't believe they have a Christmas tree. As I look around the room at my students, I see stereotypes collapsing under the delicate weight of the very real presence of this caring and animated writer sharing her life and her work with us all.

In their last short paper of the course, students return to our opening reading in the anthology *Race, Class, and Gender* and to the concept of "an inclusive perspective" (Andersen & Collins, 2007). Focusing on readings and films in our exploration of multiethnic and Arab American lives and issues, students examine how the combined factors of race or culture, class, gender, *and* sexual orientation affect the ability of any two individuals or characters to construct a full and meaningful life in the United States—and the meaning of their findings (Appendix B).

L.A. Life/American Life

Our last images in this course emerge from the homes and streets of L.A., where one after another Americans from the multiple cultures that make up this nation crash into each other and try to make sense of their lives. The film *Crash* (Haggis, 2005) enables students to pull together observations and responses that have emerged in our weeks together—about the needs, frustrations, and quandaries of individuals and the collisions across cultures that happen daily in this country; about how confusing that can sometimes be; about the power of stereotypes and the power of ignorance; and about our living our lives so separate from each other that it's hard to know where to begin to close the gaps in our understanding of each other.

While students watch *Crash* in class, they work outside of class on the final paper in the course—exploring any issue of race, culture, class, gender, or sexual orientation through multiple perspectives grounded in course materials and drawing conclusions from their findings (Chapter 5 and Appendix B). Our last day together consists of our sharing a multicultural potluck brunch and the theses and findings of their papers. And then, after hugs and good wishes all around, they are gone. The final quietness of the room is too quiet, too empty, always.

Our journey has been, on some days, intense. Sometimes our discoveries have strained our relationships; other days they have brought us closer together. It's been a good journey, though, one we'll remember.

READING ACROSS CULTURES, EXAMINING THE LIVES OF MEN AND WOMEN: A PEDAGOGY OF MULTICULTURALISM

Several choices have informed our cross-cultural journey and given it meaning for these students. Together, these choices serve the needs of the students and their society.

Texts and films reflect the multicultural nature of American society; its scholarship, literature, and films; and the community in this classroom. Students see themselves and others, as well as issues that concern them, reflected in these works, and thus these works are able to engage them in reading, analytical thinking, writing and addressing complex social issues. These works help students feel less alone. They invite questions that are not easy to ask. They clear up confusion. They also enable students to see themselves through others' eyes; this, in turn, leads to greater self-awareness—of thoughts, words, and actions.

Rather than negate the complexity of the microcosm of a multicultural society in the classroom and the challenges of addressing multisided, sensitive, and tenaciously difficult issues, these works enable us to embrace them. They reward multiple bases and types of knowledge. Students bring multiple perspectives to bear on each of these works, and with those multiple perspectives come layers of healthy debate and greater understanding of each other and these issues.

These texts place the concerns of writers and artists of color—men and women—into the center of learning. Such study helps prepare students for the coming minority majority, the coming White minority—and, within us all, an accompanying shift in a sense of self.

Many of these writers and their concerns have, over the years, been as cast out of the educational and artistic mainstream, as students from these cultures in past decades have been cast out from American schools. Writers of color have been told by publishers and academics to "get rid of" the stuff of life that vitalizes their art. Many of these writers and the issues at the heart of their work are still neglected in course reading lists. The writers who have been silenced—and the fact of such silencing—are important for students to know.

Our reading across America acquaints students with a range of ways of thinking about issues of gender within the context of race and culture. Students move from thinking about individual men's and women's senses of self, possibilities, and restrictions within a given culture, to beginning to understand the impact of larger forces within and across multiple cultures that affect the sense of self and the self-realization of men or women. Students see, in the individuals and characters they meet, the power of resistance and self-expression, strength, determination, and success in the face of factors that serve to constrict them. Students also see actions that have been taken on the part of those in power that were so sweeping that individuals who were the victims of these actions could never fully repair the damages to their lives as men or women.

Our approaches to these works engage students in building a wide range of skills in reading, critical thinking, writing, speaking, and listening. As students explore works of literature and crucial issues across cultures, they gain experience in reading and analyzing multiple forms of texts, exploring multiple perspectives, engaging in multisided discussions, and writing within a multicultural context. They read research, theory, and statistics as background for literature and films. They explore the expressive forms of nonfiction and fiction, the scholarly essay, personal essay, short story, novella as interlocking vignettes, novel as allegory, and the graphic novel; they explore comedy and satire, as well as feature and documentary film as art or social commentary. Students also explore, in multiple ways, their own responses to these works—as leaders or participants in discussions; through individual presentations; through personal writing in course journals; and through analytical writing in short papers, a midterm exam, and a final paper.

The voices in these texts and films and our own voices called forward in discussing them create an "embryonic democracy" (Parker in Frank, 2001) in the classroom, fuller and richer than we could be without them. In front of us, these writers and filmmakers become models of engaged citizens, and the individuals and characters they describe bring us knowledge of a broader America than any of us could know without them.

CONCLUSION

Students leave this course having experienced a sense of the human dimension and the formal complexity—the art—at the core of many works across multiple cultures. They have become more thoughtful readers, writers, and discussants, as well as better listeners. They are beginning to understand the need for cross-cultural interactions across our nation to be different than they have been so often in the past. They are beginning to understand the need to employ a multicultural perspective in their thinking, speaking, writing, and living. Texts and films trigger responses on the part of students that range from tears and laughter, to an analysis of the workings of a text or film, to thinking about national policy. They are on their way to becoming a more informed electorate. This is the power and beauty of focusing on issues of race, culture, and gender in texts and films across multiple American cultures in the classroom—on the part of scholars, writers, and artists, and on the part of our students. Magic happens in these moments.

Reading Literature and Films Through the Lens of Class: Breaking Taboos, Examining Factors That Influence Class Membership and Mobility

Class matters.

—bell hooks, *Where We Stand: Class Matters*

Class realities are denied, deflected, mystified.

—Paul Lauter and Ann Fitzgerald, *Literature, Class, and Culture*

INTRODUCTION: CLASS IN STUDENTS' LIVES/CLASS IN ART

"Ms. D., Ms. D., it's class! It's class!" T. says, running into the room breathless. T. is an ebullient, electrically alive, and animated young woman who lives her life in two cultures on two sides of the world. Born in this country, she regularly spends long periods of time in Israel, deeply connected to life there with her extended family. She has dual citizenship. If she returns now, she will need to spend time in the Israeli army. Her family opposes this, but she is torn. She wants to be in Israel, but she also wants to attend college in the United States. Already a young emissary, she spends afternoons working in a community group dedicated to bringing together young Arabs and Jews. She can imagine a life in international relations. She wants to be able to take care of her parents, who have given her so much, and, for many reasons, she wants to serve in the Israeli army. As warm and animated as she is, she has been lonely here. And she has not been able to figure out why. In our opening days together, the film *School Colors* (Andrews, 1994) has made her cry—the kids so segregated, so apart, she explains later, even dividing themselves into separate graduations by culture. The day she literally runs into the room, she has just been thinking about our initial images and readings on class. This, she says, is why she has felt alone. Suddenly, many moments of her young life here make sense. In her emerging awareness of the impact of class divisions on her own day-to-day life, young T. is not alone; but as with many of her classmates, class has had the power to make her feel alone. Even beyond the power of her ongoing identification with lives lived on the other side of the world, it is class divisions here that have, overridingly, made her feel alone.

As with all students, class membership and class divisions encircle the students in this classroom like the air they breathe. It affects their lives outside of school and follows them in the door of their school each morning. And it affects their coming together in the classroom. Yet they have very little help in understanding or interpreting multiple dimensions of class in their lives. The works of American writers and filmmakers across cultures are also infused with the marks of class, and their stories can enable us to better understand this aspect of our lives. As with all good works of art, literature and films can illuminate and clarify our own and others' lives, help us understand factors that shape those lives, and enable us to feel less alone and confused. They can offer us ways of thinking and acting as we chart the paths of our own lives. So in this classroom we read literature and films through the lens of class.

SCHOOLING AND CLASS

Much has been made in recent years about the widening gap between the rich and the poor in America, a new Gilded Age that has seen spectacular accumulation of wealth among the wealthiest 1%, while over 17% of all children live in poverty (National Poverty Center, 2006). Further, "though we usually think of segregation in racial and ethnic terms, it's important to also realize that the spreading segregation has a strong class component" (Orfield & Yun, 1999, p. 3).

Ours is a school community and a classroom reflecting the imbalanced distribution of privilege and power in the United States. Students whom the sociopolitical system and their schooling have served well and students whom the sociopolitical system and schools prior to this school may or may not have served well learn alongside each other. Their lives outside of school take them down different neighborhood streets. Many do not know upclose each other's worlds; they often do not travel into each other's homes and neighborhoods, in part because of class differences. Every day, our students live out the effects of class divisions in modern-day America, and this creates divisions among them in a classroom.

THE POWER, BONDS, AND CHASMS OF CLASS
THROUGH ADOLESCENT EYES

These adolescents are not naive to the presence and power of class that surrounds them, and their observations are consistent with many findings in contemporary research on class and schools. Entering the classroom, many of these students have a broad awareness of the effects of class in their daily lives—on their own lives, on the lives of members of their families, on the lives of their peers, in the workings of their school and their neighborhoods, and at the heart of issues that surround them in their society.

Their awareness of class may begin at home. Their individual assumptions, wishes, and dreams are in part carved out of the knowledge of their family's financial freedom or constraint. Some students carry an awareness of a wide range of opportunities for themselves and their families; others, an awareness of financial challenges. For one Black student, this came as she left school for part-time jobs that had her working late into the night as well as on weekends to help out financially at home. Students also see family members' lives reflect the effects of class in this often fast-paced and unforgiving economic environment. For one White student, this meant watching his grandmother lose her job when she was unable to work a new cash register and his hoping she could find another job if she kept looking.

They are also aware of class divisions in the workings and daily life of their school. Part of their knowledge of each other comes from the evidence of relative levels of purchasing power they hear discussed in the locker rooms or see played out in front of them. It colors their assumptions and their expectations. It shapes their social lives; at times it dictates inclusion and exclusion. It makes and interrupts groups. At times, discussions among those who are financially comfortable have resulted in students who do not share those advantages creating a wholly fictional narrative about their own family's financial status—and the truth of their economic situation emerging in painful ways over time. For one young Black woman, the lack of understanding among peers of class realities beyond their own was very vivid: "I know that my classmates don't understand what it means to work and have nothing to show for it. I often think people at school think it's so easy to just 'quit' or 'get a new job.' It's not, because life is complicated when you don't have money."

These students also see class dynamics shape every step of their route beyond high school: what they can reasonably hope for or not, including college or university life; or their relationship to the standardized tests that loom between them and a college of their choice, the results for which, in the minds of students across class lines, are tied directly to the ability to purchase higher results through expensive tutoring. They experience class pressures in the tensions and rivalries that can emerge as universities send out admission letters and in the options, tied ultimately to financial resources, that are available to them.

And they see class at work in their larger world. For some students, this means an awareness of privilege and a dependency on a privileged way of life to sustain their image of themselves. Other students are acutely aware of the power of class over their own and others' lives and its power to create divisions among them. Some of those divisions are clear in the segregated neighborhoods that surround them in this major American city. One young Black woman mourned the state of a poor Black neighborhood: "While I was on the bus today, on California, I looked around me and saw debris all over the bus. I looked out the window and saw garbage all over the streets. I noticed that all the people on the bus and on the streets were Black. I felt an extreme sadness for my people because it all looked so hopeless."

They also cast their eye at the convergence of race and class and opportunity. This young Black woman described a clear sense of the lack of equal opportunity she sees around her tied to racial identity: "At every single group [job] interview that I've done, all of the people have been people of color. How are people of color expected to go to school, work, take care of families, and still fight to climb the corporate ladder that's so easily accessible to other people. It's unreal!"

Despite the sweeping awareness of the effects of class that surround these students, their understanding of the concept of class varies. This statement captured one White student's uncertainties:

What is class? Until this year, I thought that people didn't talk about it, that it was archaic and something left over from a long time ago. I don't know where I fit in the "class system," and I'm not sure if there are even defined lines. I also don't understand the importance of class or whether the fact that I am beginning to understand what it means is good. I guess that I shouldn't turn a blind eye to it if it's there; however, is it just going to be another way for me to categorize people?

All of these students are attempting to live with what they are discovering of the nature and power of class in their own lives and in the lives of others, but that is not always easy. In response to seeing the documentary film *School Colors* (Andrews, 1994), about the senior class at Berkeley High School, one young Black woman explained: "I believe there is a lot to be said for someone who acknowledges his own social class in relation to others. I have always struggled with my social class." For one young White woman, uneasiness came after an uncomfortable dialogue with a friend of color: "There was suddenly this tension between us, like, I felt guilty for being rich, and he felt ashamed of being poor. It revealed to me why people of different socioeconomic groups are so segregated. It's this horrible tension that no one wants to face."

Thus, many students have a persistent comforting or discomforting awareness of class without a larger understanding that could give them a greater sense of clarity as they move about, build relationships, make decisions, and take action in their world.

CLASSED LIVES IN AMERICAN LITERATURE

Although all students are affected by the impact of class, it is little studied and discussed in the context of their schools, especially in relation to the study of literature. In their collection of readings, *Literature, Class, and Culture*, Lauter and Fitzgerald (2001) have observed that "class deeply affects how we see ourselves and others" (p. 7), and yet class realities are rarely addressed except in economics courses, which largely focus on the workings of business: "Even in classrooms, many people seem afraid to talk about class, whatever their own might be; such conversation often raises awkward and embarrassed silences" (p. 2).

Additionally, although class is tied to how all students experience their world, class membership has been unequally represented in classroom texts that make up course reading lists. The (traditionally White) canon of American literature has been dominated by texts written by comfortable members of the upper class. As the American literary canon was biased from its inception toward the East Coast and White writers, so it was biased toward the gentry until the 20th century. Within the traditional (White) literary canon, Mark Twain threw open the doors on working-class American characters and ushered in the works of such writers as Edgar Lee Masters, Sherwood Anderson, Upton Sinclair, and Carl Sandburg, whose writing captured modest lives and the exploited worker. But even these writers were capturing the lives of the working class from the perspective of the middle class, lacking an authenticity of voice. The works of writers of color—works which *were* often exploring the lives of the working class from positions originating across the class spectrum (when they could get published and distributed)— have been visibly and broadly kept off classroom reading lists (Applebee, 1993). The ripple effects of the civil rights movement and the gradual, growing recognition and embrace of writers of color, in part through an emerging focus on multicultural education, began opening up the canon and the classroom to writers of color and to writers emerging from the continuum of class. Still, however, few writers from the working class hold places on course reading lists. Literature courses have remained largely the domain of White writers writing from the perspective of the comfortable. This deprives all students from learning about the broad range of powerful American writers, the broad range of American lives across class lines, and the workings of class; and it prohibits working-class students from being able to identify with texts that reflect the realities of their lives.

Such practices within public discourse or in the classroom have a number of effects. Many of our students experience the impact of class individually and alone, and this can make them feel isolated, frustrated, hurt, confused, sometimes angry, sometimes guilty. This serves to perpetuate their questions and confusions. Over time, to the extent that they have few opportunities to discuss the nature and impact of class divisions in this country, such silence leaves them ill equipped to understand dynamics that shape their own and others' lives, creates distances among them across class lines, and leaves them unexposed to thinking that could eventually prepare them to vote on policies that support their own lives and the life of the broader community. Such lack of knowledge serves the interests of the powerful and maintains the status quo.

Within this larger context, the study in this classroom seeks to explore the nature and implication of class in individual and group lives through the works of significant American scholars, writers, and artists (Appendix B).

A CURRICULUM AND PEDAGOGY OF CLASS: CROSSING THE LINES OF CLASS IN A CLASSROOM

Reading, Discussing, and Writing About Class

On a screen at the front of the room, a camera takes us out onto the streets of Chicago and beyond, where we hear the voices of men and women: stranded survivors of Hurricane Katrina, with no resources, calling for help. A vivacious young woman driving a BMW, a gift she says, as she explains: "I consider myself middle class. I'm a cocktail waitress with no education, and I feel like I get a lot of disrespect because of what I do." The camera next moves back and forth between two families—one living in a modest neighborhood in Chicago, another in an affluent suburb. We hear the mothers talking about schools, family activities, parenting, discipline. What becomes clear is that this is an investigation into class and the ways it has influenced the lives, values, and choices of individuals and families. We hear from Robert Reich, professor of public policy at the University of California–Berkeley, as he describes the narrowing of the middle class and how that translates into the day-to-day experiences of those who dream of climbing the American ladder. We also hear from the grown children of two of America's wealthiest families: an heir to the Johnson & Johnson fortune, who has distanced himself from his family through making a documentary film on the moneyed class, and a granddaughter of Warren Buffett, who describes growing up within not only the ease of wealth but also the belief held by her grandfather that his grandchildren would be provided enough money for their educations but would be expected thereafter to build lives on their own (Winfrey, 2006).

We establish the lens of class early on in this course in a segment called "'Equal Opportunity' in a 'Classless Society': Myth or Reality"—just before we begin reading across multiple cultures (Chapter 2). We thus provide students with a framework for examining, through this perspective, lives we will meet throughout the remainder of the course. For our purposes, we define class as "a position in a society's hierarchy based on income, education, occupation, or neighborhood" (Jandt, 2007, p. 16). Through the clips from Oprah's *Class in America* (Winfrey, 2006), students are immediately engaged in recognizing moments parallel to their own family lives and moments in lives very different from their own. The clips provide an animated, engaging, and safe focal point, with plenty of familiar terrain for beginning a discussion of this sensitive aspect of our lives.

Our study moves next to several first-person perspectives on class from writers across multiple cultures, including reflections on the lure and trade-offs of successful upward mobility, and a scholarly essay on the very real challenges standing in the way of upward mobility.

The three personal narratives come from individuals in three different cultures, each of whom has made the journey upward through American ranks of class. Although these individuals' experiences in many ways embody the possibility and the model of upward mobility so touted in this society, we learn quickly of the challenges that may accompany that journey and of the losses as well as the gains along the way. In "Coming to Class Consciousness," her personal meditation on class, bell hooks (2000) shares her experiences as she moves from life in her family home in the poor, rural, segregated South onto the campus of a women's college in the South, where she faces intense isolation for reasons of race and class, and, from there, to Stanford University, where, as a transfer student, she experiences her first encounter with the Black elite and various ways in which those in the upper class, Black and White, may—or may not—try to connect with a woman who is poor and Black. Richard Rodriguez (1982) describes what he experienced in his rise from working-class Latino roots in Sacramento, California, to Stanford student, educator, scholar, and writer: the growing alienations from home, family, and language. And Linda Glennon (2001), a White sociologist, takes us into her childhood growing up working class in the shadows of the Gothic buildings of Yale University and the moments of deepening understanding about the ways in which she and other "townies" were viewed, exploited, and dismissed, socially or sexually, by the then all-young-men in the rarified halls and private clubs of Yale.

All students are asked to read bell hooks's work and then to read one of the additional works. We discuss hooks's work as a class; the next day, students break into smaller groups for student-led conversations on the thinking of either Richard Rodriguez or Linda Glennon. For each work, our conversations focus on the moments in these lives that led each of these individuals to an awareness of class; the factors, inner and outer, that enabled them to move upward through the American class hierarchy; and the impact of that journey that each faced along the way.

As with any text, these texts speak to each of these students uniquely, depending on the students' own lives and experiences. One unusually powerful aspect of these particular narratives is that they speak directly, although in different ways, to students from a variety of classes. For one young Black woman, bell hooks's "Coming to Class Consciousness" became a seminal text in a semester of reading. "Oh my gosh, Ms. D.!" she calls out coming into class the day we will discuss these pieces, "I underlined every sentence in this reading. Everything she said, I could identify with." I give her hooks's book for her own library; within days, she has read every essay in the collection. It is for her a book to hold on to, a book that has spoken directly to her life. Several young White students, removed from hooks's position through both race and class, find it hard to understand why she stays at Stanford: "If there was so much she didn't like there, why did she stay?" The imaginative leap across class lines required from their own positions of financial comfort to bell hooks's perspective means that it is very difficult for them to fully appreciate the challenges involved in hooks's journey—especially within the ongoing and mythical power of the American Dream. Other White students immediately identify with the students at Yale and their impact on those in the environs of New Haven with fewer options. For one young White man in the process of looking at a number of colleges, the essay caused him to re-see himself through others' eyes—as an intruder. The three personal narratives address multiple positions of these students' own class memberships: They speak to many students who relate directly to the experiences of the authors, they speak to other students familiar with the worlds represented by Yale and Stanford, and they vividly depict the collision of classes in the environments of schools—something all of these students can relate to.

With these personal essays as our base, we move next to a scholarly essay and meditation on the workings of class, especially within the institutions and structures that exert force on the trajectory of an individual life. In her essay "Tired of Playing Monopoly?" Donna Langston (2007) describes the cultures that accompany specific classes and examines the very real factors that stand in the way of upward mobility for a White, working-class, single mother who eventually comes to see such a dream as embodying no more control or predictability for an individual than does playing a game of Monopoly.

Having established this lens for examining class issues in the texts and films that will make up the remainder of the course, we begin our journey across America (Chapter 2), meeting, in fiction, nonfiction, and films, lives nestled in multiple cultures across the country. As we meet characters in literature or feature films or real individuals whose voices fill scholarly and personal essays and documentary films, we interrogate their situations not only from the perspectives of race, culture, and gender but also from the perspective of class. What is their class situation as we meet them? Are they comfortably situated financially? If so, what is the background of their having arrived in that position? Are they struggling financially, and if they are, are they able to move upward in America? If so, what factors enable that? If not, what factors make that difficult or impossible? We look at such individual, environmental, and structural factors as family income and circumstances at birth, continued availability of financial support, family support, schooling, motivation, wishes, drives, self-concept or self-confidence, health, relationship to work, availability of jobs, unemployment levels, individuals surrounding them, native language, discrimination, institutional racism, and policies and practices in private industry and government. Eventually we are able to ask ourselves: How are the class boundaries of America constructed? What are the inner and outer factors that support or inhibit the building of financially secure lives? What are the personal, structural, or institutionalized factors at work in shaping these lives?

A glance at a few of the lives we meet gives some idea of our exploration. The documentary film *Children of the Harvest* (Court & Arango, 1998), shown as background for Tomas Rivera's (1992) famous novella on migrant workers *And the Earth Did Not Devour Him*, introduces us to the Flores family, Mexican American citizens attempting to earn a living as migrant laborers. At a far remove from this family, yet controlling their experiences, are the discrepancy between laws governing children working in industry or retail and in agriculture; the price-setting mechanisms that determine this family's income, no matter how hard the family works and how many children forfeit an education to help make the family's daily income; and the paucity of inspectors whose purpose is to prevent exploitation of underage workers. No amount of hard work, honesty, integrity, and love will elevate this family out of poverty, nor will how many of their children leave school to work beside them in the fields. In Maria Ripoll's (2004) film *Tortilla Soup*, an affluent, loving Latino widower provides a warm and caring base from which to launch his three daughters into successful careers. Born to a family of modest means, fictional Harvard-educated African American Pierre de la Croix in Spike Lee's (2001) film *Bamboozled* writes for a major television network, but ultimately power at the highest levels fuels corporate decisions that render impossible his dreams of creating television programs with healthy images of middle- and upper-class Black Americans, and his dreams eventually destroy him. And in *The Cats of Mirikitani* (Hattendorf, 2008), we see Executive Order 9066 eliminate economic opportunities for Japanese Americans for a prolonged period of time through their internment on the West Coast during World War II.

In some of these works, we see the advantages of birth; in some, we see hard work bring rewards; and in some, we watch individuals struggle against powerful forces that make impossible the gains they seek through the fruits of their labor. In a number of these works of art, invisible, structural, institutionalized factors serve to overwhelm all individual attempts to climb the American ladder of upward mobility. Policies related to the minimum wage, child labor, and immigration—and, in some cases, racism institutionalized at the highest levels of private industry and government—render impossible in one way or another the dreams of success grounded in integrity and hard work for these individuals and their families.

Students further wrestle with these complex issues through their discussions with each other. The following excerpt of a discussion is taken from a conversation that emerged after a day of tension fueled by some students not taking seriously the conditions facing the migrant workers in *And the Earth Did Not Devour Him* and other students withdrawing from the conversation out of frustration and hurt. The lives and struggles of migrant families are very close to some of these students whose extended family members or relatives have worked in the fields and far removed from others of these young urbanites. This discussion among young Jewish American, African American, White, Israeli American, and Latino students became a debate about the possibility—and the price—of upward mobility:

N. (White male): My grandfather was very poor. He got out for a higher class.

M. (White male): It's easy—there are so many stories.

J. (White male): I disagree. There are many barriers.

C. (Latina): See, where M. is coming from, it seems possible. But the stories are [about] a very, very small percentage. They worked their asses off and pushed everything else out of life. Everybody works hard, but only the best of them will get there.

M. (White male): The people, like, really desire it.

K. (African American female): I agree that opportunities now are better and a small percentage will make it. The problem is that opportunity [can exist] and people don't know it. Kids that grow up in the ghetto, public housing, poor schools don't know they can get over, there's another world out there. The problem is getting over the [boundaries] in your house or neighborhood or school. A kid [at our school] says to me: "At school I have to talk proper, but at home my brother makes fun of me." [This child]'s trying to manage two separate worlds—you can have a mental breakdown. It's hard to balance two different worlds.

T. (Israeli American female): I disagree [with M.], too. It's hard to move up in class without giving up who you are. You leave certain things behind. You have to sacrifice so much—family, culture.

J. (White male): Is it worth what you can get by leaving sacrifices behind?

S. (White male): Can you make it without conforming to the White middle class?

J. (White male): You can't succeed without conforming.

S. (White female): I think it's luck.

A. (Jewish American male): It's a paradox. It's harder to figure out your place in society after college. Maybe [I'll have] luck and a good job. Or how much do I return to family and origins and contradict how I see myself? It's hard to lead both lives side by side.

Their observations suggest some sense of a wide range of salient issues: the persistence of the American Dream, the illusion that individual hard work can ensure success, the role of luck, and the awareness or lack of awareness of the challenges and potential losses facing individuals attempting upward mobility. Their conversations, however, allow all these students to come together from across multiple lines of class to learn from each other's divergent perspectives and to wrestle out their contrasting assumptions, observations, questions, and confusions grounded in the personal experiences and wisdom of their own lives.

In addition to readings, films, and discussions, students also process the complexities of class through their writing. Many choose to share their thoughts informally in their course journals, for which they must write two entries a week on any issue of race, culture, class, gender, or sexual orientation. The focus of the second short paper in the course requires that students examine the lives of Latino characters from multiple socioeconomic classes in the context of factors that support or inhibit upward mobility, examine the discrepancies between Latino stereotypes and the real lives of Latinos and the impacts of those differences, link a scholarly essay on class to one of two personal essays by writers across multiple cultures, or craft their own personal essay entitled "Coming to Class Consciousness" in the mode of bell hooks's essay of that same title. They are also asked to collect their thoughts about class on the midterm exam and, at the end of the course, to use class as one dimension of applying Andersen and Collins's (2007) concept of an inclusive perspective to the analysis of two lives—real or fictional—they encountered in the last two segments of the course (Appendix B).

A few excerpts give an idea of the range of their thinking as young writers:

One young White student noticed the effect of taking part in our own school's program of community engagement on his understanding of class division. His observation bears an uncanny understanding of the power of class identity and position passed on at home from parents to children and described by researchers: "Without these experiences [in community engagement], people of the upper class will not be willing to give up anything in order to cease the plight of the lower class and impoverished. They will hold tightly onto their rung on the ladder of class at all costs until their children are old enough to take their place."

Several students show savvy thinking about the impact of the American media's messages about class—laden with stereotypes—in the absence of formal education of the young about this aspect of their lives. One White student wrote: "Growing up as a kid, no one lays out the hierarchy of American society. They don't teach it to you in school or in textbooks; it is something that you pick up from social references in television, movies, radio, and all sorts of media."

Here a young Latino decries the lingering illusion most Americans continue to nurture and a pervasive trap for the poor: "Most Americans believe there is no class system. This is not true, it is very prevalent and it goes a long way in determining how your life will turn out. Even though people work two jobs they cannot get ahead. The system is set up so that only those with education can do well, but the people in poverty cannot afford a good education."

What makes it possible for these students from diverse backgrounds to come together and wrestle with some of the toughest and most uncomfortable issues influencing their lives as they look back on childhood and forward toward lives of independence? First is the need for us, their teachers, to understand something of the class dynamics our students may be experiencing.

Understanding the Students in Front of Us

As students from multiple classes come together in a classroom, all of them bring with them teachings, assumptions, values, experiences, and behaviors tied to class; these will make our coming together more complex and more challenging but ultimately more broadly and vitally instructive. Recent research on education and social class can help us understand more about the

students who join us from across class lines. Such research confirms many of
the observations made by my own students over the years as well as dynamics apparent in the daily life of our schools.

Class stratification in homes is re-created in school. Higher-income
families mobilize resources within the school to ensure their children are
well served and can carry forward social and cultural capital into the next
stage of their lives. Lower-income families feel less comfortable interacting
with school officials (Brantlinger, 1993).

Broadly, even within schools desegregated by class, higher-income and
lower-income students are still segregated throughout their experiences in
school: Each group self-segregates, and each group experiences schooling
within the context of class background (Brantlinger, 1995).

Higher-income students form cliques with other higher-income students. For higher-income students, school is a "privileging experience"
(Brantlinger, 1995), and they move through multiple aspects of it with a level
of comfort and ease. They come into school assuming that, through their
privileged position, they can exclude students of lower status (Brantlinger,
2007; Van Galen, 2007). The cost of affluence for these students, however,
includes the need to hold on to their position and power; pressure to succeed; anxiety over meeting the demands of their parents as well as their own
demands; worries; and, at times, arrogance or insecurity, anger or depres-
sion. Such pressures result in these students "casting Others as outsiders"
(Brantlinger, 2007, p. 244).

Lower-income students also form cliques with others of similar class
backgrounds. But unlike their higher-income classmates, lower-income students experience stress in many aspects of their schooling, every day. Privilege is visible, and the privileged hold on to privilege. This in turn renders
working-class students as "outsiders," bringing them humiliation and exclusion (Brantlinger, 1995, 2007; Van Galen, 2007). Lower-income students
are overrepresented in lower-tracked and in special education classes and
must confront negative images that accompany such placements. Lower-
income students must confront images tied to their involvement or not in
extracurricular activities. And they face perceived rejections by their peers
and teachers. These negative experiences at school, which are so different
from their wishes for their schooling, result in stress and anger as well as
feelings of rejection and vulnerability (Brantlinger, 1995). These students already know "the hidden injuries of class" (Sennett & Cobb, 1993). Students
from lower-income backgrounds must also contend with the conflicted feelings associated with placing themselves on a path of upward mobility. Effective schooling can give these students significant skills and capital for
later life, and through their schooling they can re-imagine their futures (Van
Galen, 2007). On this path, however, they will face considerable challenges

in maintaining close ties with those they are leaving behind (Hurst, 2007). Despite such challenges facing lower-income students in schools desegregated by class, one study has shown that the majority of parents of lower-income students want their children to be in such schools. Such schools, the parents maintained, were usually better schools. Yes, they acknowledged, their children would experience challenges in interacting with the children of privilege, but such interactions would prepare them for what they would encounter in their later lives, and they would get "a better education" (Brantlinger, 1985).

In the majority of our students, their understanding about class will be grounded in two illusions. (1) There are two classes: the rich and the poor. (2) Class is most essentially tied to individual effectiveness or failings: Wealth comes from "motivation, education, and taking advantage of others," and poverty results from "laziness and dropping out of school." Fewer than half understand the role of "inheritance and chance" in the creation of wealth or the role of the lack of jobs and high unemployment in the creation of poverty (Brantlinger, 1995, pp. 1–4). Their isolation from each other will continue to nourish inaccurate stereotypes and uninformed views of each other; these in turn will deepen their distances from each other—and these distances and dynamics will follow them into our classrooms.

Such powerful and complex daily class dynamics in schools mean that students need us to understand some of the factors that have influenced their lives, interactions, and needs to this point.

Establishing a Climate of Trust for the Contemplation of Literature and Films Through the Lens of Class

In addition to understanding our students, we need to establish a trusting environment within the classroom. Several practices make that possible.

The goal in this classroom is for each student to feel at home. There is an effort to ensure that each student feels that his or her voice is a significant voice, despite, too often, the reconstitution of society's class stratification—and accompanying levels of perceived power—within our schools. This classroom provides an environment where each student's experiences, wisdom, and ways of knowing are cherished for expanding the wisdom and thoughtfulness of us all. All of these students should come to know that it is the uniqueness of their own life experiences and perspectives as well as the commonality of the experiences they share with others that make them who they are and that will make them valued as thinkers, speakers, or writers as we build a community in our time together. Our discussions invite in the stories of the challenges, the joys, the concerns, and the questions of each of their young lives. As writers, they draw on the power of their observations and personal experiences as well as on the power of analysis and critical thinking.

As we move through texts and films, there is an effort to ensure that all of these students feel the comfort of insiders being addressed from a world that they know, even while being asked to enter worlds that are unfamiliar and thus expand their ways of thinking and being in the world. There is an effort to select texts and films that speak to all of these students: those whose uncertainties emerge from holding on to economic power they have already inherited; those who fear losing even the fragile foothold they have; and those whose uncertainties emerge from their nascent movement along the complex journey of upward mobility, of leaving aspects of one class behind and confronting the challenges of assimilating—or not—into another, of being asked to live in two worlds and to try to bring those worlds together.

Essential in our time together is the importance of social learning. The heterogeneity of these students' lives and backgrounds provides the opportunity for all of them to learn not only from the texts and films before them but also, perhaps even more importantly, from each other. To facilitate their vibrant and active learning from each other as well as their feeling of being individually supported, the tone valued in this room is one of respect and caring, an advocacy for each individual in our group. Our emphasis is on cooperation and support, a sharing of perspectives and ideas, and gradually, through that process, a building of meaningful communication and relationships across lines of culture and class.

Creating an Inclusive Curriculum

Crucial, too, is an inclusive curriculum. Several values guide my selection of texts and films and the process of overseeing the students as they read, screen, discuss, or write about them.

Readings and films reflect lives and experiences across multiple segments of the class spectrum so that all students can see lives that resemble their own and can begin to gain an understanding of lives different from their own.

Texts or films about particular socioeconomic groups emerge from voices within those groups rather than from voices outside of those groups. Thus, there is an effort to see that materials reflect the reality—rather than the stereotypes—of individuals and groups in multiple socioeconomic classes.

Readings and films reflect aspects of both power and vulnerability for individuals in each class, therefore suggesting the importance of knowing multiple aspects of class experiences and perspectives.

Materials facilitate greater understanding of factors that lie within and beyond the control of individuals or groups and that affect multiple directions of movement along the class spectrum, allowing students to begin to understand the complex range of factors at work in shaping class divisions and class mobility.

Additionally, I ask myself a series of questions about the ways in which students from multiple classes might respond to each of these texts and films, and doing so shapes my decisions about works to use and how to approach them.

> Do I have some sense of the types and range of responses the work might generate, and how I might oversee those responses in order to enable all students to feel included and supported in their learning?
>
> Is there a reasonable level of trust and comfort with communication within the group: between adult and students, and among students?
>
> What might be the responses of and the impact on those who are often considered the least powerful in the class spectrum, who are potentially the most vulnerable in a socioeconomically heterogeneous community, and who may know the subject most fully out of the wisdom of lived experiences in multiple worlds?
>
> What might be the responses of and the impact on those who are often considered the most powerful in the class spectrum, who are potentially the most powerful in a socioeconomically heterogeneous community, and who may know the least about lives lived differently than their own?
>
> Does the focus of study avoid distancing, voyeurism, and objectification of individuals or groups? Will some students feel exposed or objectified for the sake of others?

Ultimately, I ask myself: Does our study facilitate—through a curriculum and pedagogy that supports each of these students—a greater understanding of the experiences of individuals and groups within multiple positions on the class spectrum?

TEACHING ABOUT CLASS: DISMANTLING ILLUSIONS, CHALLENGING THE BONDS OF CLASS

What are the results of our focus on the workings of class through texts and films?

In this classroom, we make aspects of class visible, tangible, approachable. Students are provided a supportive forum for reading about class; sharing their questions, observations, and concerns in discussions; and writing about class. Our forum answers some of their questions and allows them to test their observations.

Such study provides students across class lines with a more inclusive experience with learning, enabling students from a broad range of classes to see themselves as well as others within the spectrum of the dynamics, the possibilities, and the pain of class in America through some of its most thoughtful writers and artists.

The lives the students encounter in these texts and films often evoke powerful responses—cries, literally at times, of recognition. Such a focus directly addresses the needs of these students to sort out their world, and this in turn deepens their interest in reading and writing.

Our engagement increases students' interest in this focus and provides them with a framework for analysis of class issues. Texts and films help students begin to understand factors related to class that lie within and beyond the control of individuals, families, and groups; factors that assist upward mobility or that impede that process; and the gains and losses that can accompany that journey. Students' growing familiarity with these factors enables them to move from nurturing illusions about the power of individualism and from preserving stereotypes about the rich and the poor, success and failure, to gaining a more realistic understanding of class dynamics. A brief glimpse at some of these students' observations suggests where our study has taken them.

For one Jewish student, one story in the documentary *Raising Cain* (Thompson, 2006)—of a boy growing up without parents and on welfare in the South Bronx who has aspirations of going to law school—presented a stark contrast with his own plans to follow in the footsteps of both parents and attend law school. The contrast between the viability of the aspirations of the young man in New York City and the viability of his own raised troubling implications about our society: "The sad juxtaposition of my future and this Latino boy's future demonstrates that not all futures are created equally. This is certainly not the America that de Tocqueville saw during his travels; we've certainly deviated from our ideals."

Two young White women questioned the validity of child labor in the context of migrant labor in the documentary film *Children of the Harvest* (Court & Arango, 1998). For one student, specific aspects of migrant labor led her to question the reality of the American Dream: "Part of me was so angry that the father was making his son work, depriving him of an education. On the other hand, I can see that they have NO choice. What this shows me is the unreality of the 'American Dream.' Maybe there aren't really opportunities to advance here in America." The other student considered multisided policy ramifications of this family's situation: "These families cannot afford to lose out on any able-bodied member of the family. I am still left with the question: Is it better to have strict child labor laws, or should the families be able to choose for themselves?"

Here a young Latino, a young White man, and a young Asian American man, respectively, contemplate what is and what could be in our society:

[The class system] is the major factor that determines what type of education we will receive, what type of job we will work in, and ultimately what type of life we can offer our children. In "The Cariboo Café" and in *And the Earth Did Not Devour Him*, we see the main characters struggle with America's class system and how it becomes almost impossible for any of the people they know to move up in the class hierarchy. The reality is that in America, although one wishes to believe otherwise, there exists a rigorous class system that makes it very difficult, for especially the poor, to get ahead and offer their children a better life than what they had.

We hear from Donna Langston, from Oprah, and Eduardo Bonilla-Silva that there is an indisputable link [among] class, race, and culture—the way you speak; the way you walk; the clothes you wear; where you eat, shop, and live are affected by all three of those [factors]. Although it is difficult to say what a solution may be to closing the racial and class gaps, it is an invaluable first step to have an understanding of their modern existence and [the way] they affect peoples' lives.

Reading Donna Langston's "Tired of Playing Monopoly," I appreciate the parallel she made between welfare for the rich and poor, which is something that needs light shed on it. There is an inherent imbalance in the system; the wealthy get breaks, the hard-working generally do not. But the only way to [create] a truly progressive learning environment or society [means] the "haves" need to share their resources with the "have nots." The intellect must be shared and the wealth must be shared. The problem with our society's understanding of these two assets is that we believe each is meant exclusively for the individual, when it should be the opposite.

The students have moved from embracing the idealization of class mobility embodied in the American Dream to a more realistic understanding of the strictures of class and the challenges of upward mobility, to a vision of what should be, and to thinking about policies that could begin to bring that vision into being. They are emerging as active citizens contemplating what exists in their society and ways in which that society could be made better.

CONCLUSION

As the values and practices described here suggest, the goal of education in this classroom is transformative rather than "reproductive" (Anyon, 2008, p. 202). Rather than reinforcing present rigid, distancing, and limiting social and economic divisions and hierarchies, the teaching in this classroom seeks to provide knowledge and skills, and a growing and shared cultural capital, that will allow all of these students not only to reach for their dreams but to begin to understand ways in which the society around them can better serve the needs of all, and, through developing a sense of their own agency, to see a role for themselves in that process. In this way, perhaps eventually we can send our students out into a less classed and more just society than the perplexingly and often unjustly and capriciously rich and rewarding, cruel and unforgiving one they have all inherited.

As encouraging as it is to see students grapple with the dilemmas of the powerful and rigid class divisions and structures that surround them, we cannot have illusions about the power of such teaching. Although these students see the effects of class all around them, they are just beginning to understand something of the ways in which class works in their lives—factors visible and invisible. The scholarship and the art we use in a course like this—the essays, literature, and films—take us into individual lives whose economic status is affected by both personal and structural factors. But in our focus we only gain glimpses of those overarching, sweeping, at times invisible and insidious structures that exert so much control over so many lives. Seeing discrimination that binds poor Black men to menial jobs in a hotel and prevents them from securing more lucrative jobs in construction in Toni Morrison's (1973) novel *Sula* does not reveal the myriad historical structures of power and institutional racism behind those moments of discrimination. The documentary film *Brothers and Others* (Rossier, 2004) exposes the violations of the private lives of struggling Arabs, Muslims, and South Asians on the East Coast after September 11, 2001, caused by the Patriot Act, but it does not go into the manipulation of information at the highest levels of government that eventually led to such acts and made them acceptable to many Americans. Even the scholarly essays give us only one glimpse at a time into a way of thinking about and analyzing class dynamics. As a lifelong student of education, how long did it take me to begin to understand the nature and implications of a force such as neo-liberalism and the potential effects of that thinking on individual lives, neighborhoods, and schools tied to the poor.

Many of our students, also, just as do many other Americans, remain deeply wedded to the notion of the power and possibility of the individual in this society, and multiple exposures to factors that negate that power little affect their beliefs. It is most likely simply too simple, too comforting, and too reassuring of their own power and possibility in an unsure world. And is it not the essence of human nature for us to sustain ourselves with both hopes and dreams and hard work? So, in a study like this, we move forward in incremental steps, opening the door a little bit at a time into another way of thinking—about aspects of students' own lives and the lives of those around them, powerful or powerless in the face of the class system in America.

Perhaps, however, precisely because of these challenges, and because of the extremes of wealth, the breadth of poverty, and the dramatically increasing distance among class divisions that in part define these students' society, it is all the more important that class and its issues become a focal point of study, conversation, debate, and writing. Our mix across class lines provides an ideal opportunity for these students to further their understanding of the nature and implications of class in their daily lives and in the fabric of American life. Such a focus is important for their future and ours, for their developing an inclusive sensibility about our world, and then taking on their role in bringing the reality of such a world into being.

Yes, T., you were right. It was class. It was class.

And in that moment of her awareness, her world had become a little more clear, a little more negotiable, and a little less full of illusions.

Gay, Lesbian, Bisexual, and Transgender Lives and Issues, Readings and Films: Countering Invisibility, Interrupting the Cycle of Homophobia

PROLOGUE

Rachel, a young lesbian, has listened quietly as classmates decried the right of gay or lesbian parents to adopt children. Stephen and Josh have hidden their shared identities as young gays. After he left for college, Satchen was beaten by his father for being gay. As a young adult, unable to accept her sexual orientation, Nan committed suicide.

In a large and tolerant city, in this school, and in other schools, many young gay, lesbian, bisexual, and transgender students, as well as the children of GLBT families, still feel alone. And it is their faces, their voices that haunt me in this diverse city and liberal school. It is their faces, their voices, their actions that tell me that whatever we are doing in our schools and classrooms, it is not enough. We are not doing enough to support these young men and women or to educate their peers about the lives and issues of gay, lesbian, bisexual, and transgender individuals. It is their faces and lives that guide me as I attempt to open up this classroom—its focal points, its texts, its discussions, and its sense of belonging so that they will no longer feel alone, walk alone, be alone.

The students who enter my classroom are surrounded by issues that affect the lives of GLBT individuals, as well as their own lives, gay or straight. A number of these emerging young adults have successfully navigated the coming-out process and, through their animated comfort with their own identity, provide comfort to many others. Other gay or lesbian students remain closeted. And still other students lead lives touched by the lives of family members, friends, or strangers who experience each day the effects of a society that far too often isolates, excludes, endangers, or fails to support the needs of GLBT members in our communities.

As my students' lives unfold, their experiences in their own lives or tied to the lives of those around them teach them something about the lives of GLBT individuals. They speak of a young lesbian ostracized by her mother's side of the family and leaving home to live with her father, finally feeling whole. They speak of a brother isolated at college and afraid of who he is.

66

They speak of hearing "that's so gay" spoken so cavalierly that the speaker cannot, must not know its weight or of being drawn to look at a cross-dresser on a city street because she looked so different. In all such moments, these students are learning, putting together the pieces of lives they see or lives they know of lived alone, in secret, or risking or invoking rejection by family and friends.

Some of these moments generate strong emotions in these students—hurt and anger, confusion and frustration: when they are caught in the middle and watch those they care about rejected by their families, when they hear gay bashing even in the Chicago neighborhood known as Boys Town, and when they see a gay friend behave in homophobic ways because of the homophobia surrounding him at home. Such moments may also generate a strong sense of injustice. They want their classmates to feel outrage at the mistreatment of gay or transgender friends they are close to; they want their classmates to support adoption by gay and lesbian parents; they want boys who commit acts of homophobic violence at another school to be appropriately punished. What they see also leads to a sense of yearning. They want their GLBT friends and family members to know love and support, to be accepted.

As students assemble such disparate pieces of life around them, they are left with unanswered questions. Their questions reflect uncertainty about identity, the coming-out process, and family life, as well as questions about personal, educational, and societal responsibility and practices in relation to the needs of gay, lesbian, bisexual, and transgender individuals.

It is my students' experiences in their daily lives, as well as their emotions, yearnings, and questions in response, that fuel their needs as they enter this classroom. As with my students' interest in a range of complex social issues, these students' concerns reflect Dewey's (1916/1966) definition of the ripeness for learning, and they are turning to us for help in clarifying and navigating their world. It was in the face of my students' very real needs and concerns that this forum was born and enables some of our most significant writers, artists, and scholars—as well as the students' own classmates—to respond to their questions (Appendix B).

INTRODUCTION: AN EVOLVING SOCIETY/A HOST OF QUESTIONS

These are students who have come of age during an era reflecting a broad range of emerging issues for gay, lesbian, bisexual, and transgender individuals as well as contradictory responses on the part of their society to those issues. They see a society moving forward on supporting the needs of GLBT individuals on some issues but blocking their rights in relation to other issues. The human rights of all students must be respected (Human Rights Resource Center, 2000), yet many schools are not safe spaces for GLBT students. The works of gay and lesbian writers and writers on gay and lesbian focal points constitute a robust thread of American literature, yet they are little studied in the wholeness of the identity of their sexual orientation. Study of gay and lesbian lives and issues has been shown to reduce homophobia (Van de Ven, 1995), yet vehement objections are hurled at teachers and administrators for working with these issues in the classroom.

Thus, for too many young gay, lesbian, bisexual, and transgender individuals, maturing into an identity they know is still broadly stigmatized results in identity development that is managed privately and alone for a prolonged period of time, influenced by negative societal and cultural values, attitudes, and pressures. Many do not feel emotionally and physically safe; they lack acceptance and inclusion. The lingering legacy of silence and invisibility also means that our students remain largely unaware of the legions of gay and lesbian writers, artists, and scholars who have gone before them. Lacking knowledge of this historical community of powerful and significant gays and lesbians in turn reinforces the perceived need for many young gays and lesbians to maintain their own silence and invisibility.

Additionally, my students—gay and straight—are observing and experiencing a recasting of the American family through gay, lesbian, bisexual, and transgender men- and women-headed families, including the nature of adult relationships and the roles of parenting—and this can be confusing to them. They are the children of traditional marriages, divorce, single parents, adoptive parents, gay and lesbian parents, single-culture families, and multiethnic families.

All of these students—gay and straight—are coming into their mature identities shaped in part by gender roles modeled in their individual cultures; attitudes toward sexual orientation within their individual cultures; the lives they have lived in their families; their emerging understanding of controversies, needs, and challenges facing gay, lesbian, bisexual, and transgender individuals; and their experiences with the life surrounding them. This means that many of these students bring to the forum contrasting expectations of their identities as young men and women, the nature of the relationships they construct, the nature of family life, as well as contrasting levels of tolerance for the lives of others.

My own gay and lesbian students are in many ways "lucky." They live in a major American city where they can find not only acceptance and a sense of belonging and community but also vital gay and lesbian neighborhoods, an annual gay pride parade, and a city that has played host to the International Gay Games. They are in a progressive school whose administrators and faculty reach out in multiple ways to ensure a sense of support and belonging for young gays and lesbians, members of gay- or lesbian-headed families, and gay and lesbian members of the faculty and staff; a school in which a number of gay or lesbian teachers and students are out; and a school whose commitment to issues of social justice surrounding gays is a priority throughout the institution. Observance of Ally Week, a Day of Silence, seminars, and assemblies with guest speakers and films extend and buttress the focal points that may emerge in course study. One such assembly included the screening of ABC's 20/20 documentary on a high school football star who comes out at school (Cooper, 2000), accompanied by a faculty member speaking on growing up with two moms. Yet, "That's so gay!" can still echo through halls and locker rooms. Some students and teachers remain closeted.

Shifting attitudes toward aspects of sexual orientation, notions of gender, and family life can significantly complicate our students' coming together in this classroom. But through our reading, discussions, and writing, through these students' own wishes to learn, their willingness to engage in this process, and their generosity of spirit with each other, this classroom offers an opportunity and a safe environment for all students to learn more about these aspects of American life and, through that, to build a fuller, more knowledgeable, and more trusting community with each other.

GAY, LESBIAN, BISEXUAL, AND TRANSGENDER AMERICAN LITERATURE: CODED LIVES, CLASSICS, AND BEST SELLERS

Beyond contradictory and confusing social patterns, these students inherit a vital tradition of gay, lesbian, bisexual, and transgender American writers. GLBT individuals are counted among our most significant American writers across multiple cultures from the colonies to the present and represented among our most revered, prize-winning, and best-selling authors. Throughout their robust history and despite repeated challenges to their sense of self, dignity, freedom, identity, and art, they have prevailed and remain for students of literature today exemplary models for the meaning and power of literature in our lives. Similar to gays and lesbians being referred to as "the invisible minority," however, the identity of many gay and lesbian American writers has, historically, been rendered invisible.

Gay, lesbian, bisexual, and transgender writers can boast a robust multicultural American literary tradition that began in texts of the colonists (Cavitch, 2004) and continues vitally today. Same-sex yearnings were evident in the 19th-century writings of Ralph Waldo Emerson, Henry David Thoreau, Herman Melville, Walt Whitman, and Oscar Wilde. Henry James, Emily Dickinson, Sarah Orne Jewett, and Willa Cather brought forward the spirit of same-sex "romantic friendships" in life or characters in the latter part of the 19th century and, in some cases, into the 20th century (Martin, 2004, p. 3). Langston Hughes, Countee Cullen, and Nella Larsen emerged from the Harlem Renaissance (Keating, 2007; Nelson, 2006). In the mid-20th century, Tennessee Williams, Truman Capote, Carson McCullers, John Cheever, and May Sarton wrote out of perspectives nurtured in the South and in upper-middle-class lives in New York and New England. James Baldwin and Alan Ginsburg took their places not only among the country's most well known writers but among the most visible and outspoken writers representing gay lives and experiences in their art. During the 1960s, Edward Albee published *Zoo Story*, and John Knowles gave us in his novel *A Separate Peace*, two boys at a New England prep school during World War II who, he later said, "were in love" (Cady, 2006, p. 7). The emerging civil rights movement, the Stonewall riots leading to the gay rights movement, and the women's movement meant lingering gains for gay and lesbian writers.

Within a historically inhospitable climate for all gay and lesbian writers, gay and lesbian writers of color have often faced broader challenges as they mediated constantly between being true to themselves and responding to deeply felt and expressed cultural values in their communities. Writers of color have often faced double or even triple discrimination in the larger society as a person of color and as a gay or lesbian. Lesbians of color describe being oppressed as women in a patriarchal society, lesbians in a homophobic and heterosexist society, and minorities in a predominantly White society (Wadsworth, 2007).

Some of these writers of color have had historical models to turn to within their cultural communities; others have faced intense isolation within their cultural communities and within the gay and lesbian community. Arthur Lipkin (1999), in his seminal work *Understanding Homosexuality, Changing Schools*, details the issues that have surrounded gays and lesbians of color. Contemporary Native American gays and lesbians may embrace the historical figure of the two-spirit person, a man-woman revered in some tribes, and in so doing can nestle their identity within a tribal tradition, a buttress against the discrimination they may face within their family and their community on the reservation. African Americans, Latinos, and Asian American gays and lesbians have each wrestled with the particular richness and challenges imposed on them by encircling cultural values. African American gays and lesbians historically have been accepted quietly in communities if they have remained low-key members of the community. Historical oppression of Black males in a White-dominant society means African American gay men have had to fend off not only the ongoing racism of White society but also images of gayness that conflict with holding onto manhood in a racist society. Latino gays and lesbians know their sexual orientations emerge within the machismo that defines the nature of Latino men as well as gender roles, the broadly held teachings of the Catholic Church, and, related to both of these powerful value systems, homophobia throughout the Latino community. This conflict is further deepened by the encircling racism of the White society. Asian American gays and lesbians have faced homophobia within their own Asian American community and the White society, an emphasis on the family over the individual in the Asian American community, as well as racism and distorting stereotypes from the White society. Jewish, Muslim, Mormon, and Christian gays and lesbians face carving out a life acceptable to their own needs while responding to or moving away from the teachings of their religious communities (Lipkin, 1999). Despite all of these challenges, writers such as Paula Gunn Allen, Audre Lorde, Gloria Naylor, June Jordan, Richard Rodriguez, Cherrie Moraga, Ana Castillo, David Henry Hwang, Dwight Okita, and Kitty Tsui, among so many others as gay, lesbian, or bisexual writers of color or as writers of color focusing on GLBT themes, have brought new visions into the literary landscape.

None of this literary history has been easy to build; it has been painful and difficult, step by step, life by life, work by work, decade by decade. Gay and lesbian lives were considered "unspeakable" (Cady, 2005, p. 1), but writers persevered. Their ability to reach an audience evolved from being "published abroad or by marginal presses or remain[ing] private and unpublished" during the early years to reaching best-seller status in the 1940s for several works (Cady, 2006, p. 1). Gay and lesbian writers continued writing and publishing works on aspects of gay and lesbian lives and experiences in the 1950s and 1960s despite the fact that "homosexuality was still largely invisible in society and chiefly vilified when it was spoken of at all" (Cady, 2006, p. 9).

Beyond the challenges facing gay, lesbian, bisexual, and transgender writers tied to their own or others' cultural values, the literature of gays and lesbians has been hobbled by centuries of intolerance, discrimination, and censorship by government, publishers, editors, and antigay activists. Ginsburg's *Howl* was "prosecuted as 'indecent' under a California law"; Baldwin's *Another Country* was "banned as obscene by the New Orleans Public Library" but later returned to circulation (Cady, 2005, p. 4). Works by gays and lesbians still face lack of acceptance and hostility. In March of 2008 in a suburb north of Chicago, a group known as the North Shore Student Advocacy called for the resignation or firing of the district superintendent, high school principal, and all teachers connected with the teaching of Tony Kushner's *Angels in America* to seniors in an Advanced Placement English literature course (Abderholden, 2008). Such actions continue to keep texts by gay and lesbian writers from students.

Regardless of such enduring, encircling constraints, the community of American gay and lesbian writers from the colonies to today has cumulatively contributed major works in all literary forms (fiction, poetry, drama, and nonfiction), as well as in the original form of the coming-out narrative, to the history of American literature. Within a history of works emerging from self-consciousness and coding to experimental forms and activism, many of these works stand as models of a range of forms or styles: the gothic novel as treatise on art of Oscar Wilde's *The Picture of Dorian Gray*, the nontraditional use of language and narrative by Gertrude Stein, the elegant use of autobiography by Paul Monette, the activist poetry of Adrienne Rich, the contemporary epistolary novel of Alice Walker's *The Color Purple*, the graphic novel as literary autobiography with Alison Bechdel's *Fun Home*, and, in the hands of many gay and lesbian writers, the coming-out story.

As writing potentially does for any writer and reader, the history of gay, lesbian, bisexual, and transgender literature in the United States reflects broadly and deeply the ways in which both writing and reading have supported lives. Writing by GLBT authors has served vital purposes for themselves, the GLBT community, and straight readers. The act of writing has served not only artistic and literary purposes but psychological and social purposes, individual and communal. From its beginning in the American colonies, evidence of gay and lesbian perspectives in texts helped others. From then until now, such writing has enabled readers to feel less alone. For writers themselves, the act of writing has helped them better understand their own lives, teach others about lives less understood or misunderstood, refute stereotypes and inaccuracies, stand up for individual rights, and raise questions about traditional concepts of gender (Beemyn, 2006). Their writing has also forged communities—readers brought together out of common needs, perspectives, experiences, challenges, and delights. Coming-out stories in particular have served individuals and built communities. Such stories say "I am" for writers and readers, and they enable writers and readers to recognize and accept themselves, especially readers living lives of isolation and fear far removed from urban centers of GLBT communities. These stories give voice and access to an often hidden life and love, providing insights into others' experiences and feelings. Such stories are acts of courage, describing who one is to oneself and others in a homophobic society (McNaron, 2005). Such stories speak the "unspeakable." They are acts of power: They enable their authors to stand up, to step forward, to speak out, to be visible.

Today, through the works of such writers as Michael Cunningham, Alison Bechdel, Paula Gunn Allen, Cherrie Moraga, Kitty Tsui, Becky Birtha, and David Leavitt, a multicultural gay and lesbian literary tradition continues to thrive.

Despite the robust nature of the gay and lesbian literary tradition in this country, few students are given the opportunity to study the works of these writers in the context of their gay and lesbian identities. As teachers who know, love, and understand the need for literature in our lives, in the face of the history of what these writers have done, can we not step forward to honor these writers, and welcome them—fully known, fully visible—into our classrooms? Can we not let these writers speak to our students out of these writers' understanding of the power of art in a writer's life, as well as what we ourselves know of the power of art to strengthen the lives and understanding of our young readers?

A host of factors compel us to rethink our relationship to gay and lesbian writers who have been central to the American literary tradition but excluded—in their full identity—from being part of the exploration of American literature in many American classrooms. Such curriculum is important not only in response to the integral role these writers have played in shaping American literature since its inception but also for the role they can play in our students' lives in classrooms and beyond as the students come to know the work of gay and lesbian American writers. For all of these reasons, we need to provide students with the opportunity to learn more about this powerful history of gay and lesbian American literature and to explore together significant works of literature by and about gay, lesbian, bisexual, and transgender Americans.

TOWARD OPENNESS AND CLARITY:
WRITERS, FILMMAKERS, AND A HIGH SCHOOL FORUM

As I look out on my own classroom, statistics tell me "approximately 5 percent of America's high school students identify as lesbian or gay, 16 percent of America's students have a gay or lesbian family member, and 72 percent know someone who is gay or lesbian" (GLSEN, 2004, p. 1). Because so many students have questions about multiple aspects of sexual orientation, we begin our work in this focus with background material, facts, and reliable theories to help them move more knowledgeably into the work of scholars, writers, and filmmakers and to discuss more thoughtfully the issues these works raise. To do so minimizes confusion as well as unintentionally ignorant or hurtful observations, questions, or remarks in our nascent dialogues about GLBT writers and artists and about issues tied to sexual orientation. Our first readings take students through an overview of key facts about sexual orientation (APA, 2009); reports on gay, lesbian, bisexual, and transgender individuals in schools (ACLU, 2001; GLSEN, 2004, 2009); a list of useful terms ("GLBTQ Terminology," 2008); several models of gay, lesbian, or transgender identity development (Cass, 1984; Coleman, 1982; Lev, 2004); a timeline of significant events in the history of gays and lesbians in America (*American Gay Rights*, 2009); famous GLB people in history (LAMBDA, n.d.); and suggestions for further reading (*Engl 3300*, 1997; Rosenbloom, 2006).

As with overseeing readings and discussions tied to any multisided and sensitive issues, most important in our work is support for each of the students before us. Discussions of any real and complex issues can trigger shyness, uncertainty, defensiveness, frustration, or anger within students. In discussions of issues tied to gay, lesbian, bisexual, and transgender individuals, straight students may initially feel shy or awkward or uncomfortable. Students with close ties to GLBT individuals in their families or among their friends may be reserved, or they may openly embrace an exploration they value for themselves and for the way in which it honors those they care about. Out GLBT students may be primarily listeners, or they may be animatedly, passionately, and openly engaged in discussing issues close to their lives. Not all gay students are out, however. Gay students who are not out may be searching for reliable information; for an opportunity to explore issues close to their lives through readings, films, and discussions; or for an environment where they know that gays and lesbians will be supported and respected. All students bring complex identities to our forum. Beyond identities related to sexual orientation, all of these students are juggling aspects of developing racial or cultural identities and class identities, they are exploring relationships to both their own culture and to other cultures based on who they are, and they are exploring who they are as young men or young women. For all of these reasons, we need to be observant about dynamics unfolding in front of us and support each of our students every step of the way in their discussions and interactions.

Our first discussion of GLBT issues follows their reading of our initial handout. I ask them why they think this focus is included in the course and why I have given them this packet of background readings. As we begin our discussions, students leap in. One student explains, "This group has been oppressed, historically and today." Others join in: "Gays are a self-identified group—like others we examine in this course." "Many issues tied to gays and lesbians are very controversial, and issues tied to gays and lesbians surround us: the rights and responsibilities of gays and lesbians, marriage, adoption, their acceptance or not within churches. We need to be able to understand these issues."

They also easily move into the information provided in a fact sheet published by the American Psychological Association (APA, 2009). Even though they have all studied this focus during a required health class their freshman year, many students admit they are still confused about sexual orientation. The fact sheet prompts so many questions, we never get beyond reading the first few facts aloud. The students seem to know that their lack of facts can lead them into uncertainty, awkwardness, insensitivity, or stereotypes. Our introductory background also includes looking at several identity development models for gay, lesbian, or transgender individuals: the Coleman (1982) five-stage model of lesbian/gay identity development, the Cass (1984) model of lesbian/gay identity development, and the Lev (2004) six-stage model of transgender emergence. Because in this course we have earlier studied theories and models of racial identity development (Chapter 2), these identity development models come into a familiar framework. Examining and talking about identity theories and models tied to sexual orientation also means that these students will move with greater understanding into reading and discussing the works of literature and films that follow, as well as into living their daily lives. Terms, too, will facilitate our learning ("GLBTQ Terminology," 2008). The vocabulary tied to sexual orientations is complex, and, as I explain to the students, knowing something about this language means we can interact more thoughtfully. "What do I call you?"— a question often applied to racial or cultural identities—has application for GLBT individuals as well.

Next we look at statistics tied to the experiences of young gays and lesbians in schools: figures on harassment, bullying, aggression, feelings of lack of safety, dropping out, and suicide (ACLU, 2001; GLSEN, 2004, 2009). We also talk about the lawsuit that one young gay student successfully brought against his public school in Wisconsin for lack of protection against harassment, resulting in a settlement for nearly $1 million. Although all of these students are familiar with the casual language of cruelty—"That's so gay!" "Faggot!"—they are startled by the figures on harassment and bullying of GLBT students in schools and by the sweeping effects of such actions on the schooling and emotional well-being of students their own age. Many have not yet connected these common and casual references to the ways in which they are experienced by many of their classmates—gay or straight.

Lastly in this introductory handout, we look at a timeline of the American gay rights movement (*American Gay Rights*, 2009) and a list of famous gay, lesbian, and bisexual individuals (LAMBDA, n.d.); the gradual emergence of gay, lesbian, bisexual, and transgender American authors from secrecy to openness over the decades; a list of classic and contemporary works by gay and lesbian authors I have adapted from one university course reading list (*Engl 3300*, 1997); and information on a new guide to gay-friendly college campuses (Rosenbloom, 2006). We linger on the importance of the Stonewall riots in New York City in 1969, a turning point in gay and lesbian American history and the beginning of the gay rights movement. Coming to this timeline in a classroom in Chicago, we note that in 1924 the Society for Human Rights in Chicago became the first gay rights organization in the country and that in 1962 Illinois became the first state to decriminalize consenting, private homosexual acts between adults.

As with conversations focused on any social issue, the thrust of this conversation varies depending on the makeup of the group. The first time I oversee this conversation, the group is 50% students of color and 50% White students. For this group, much of the conversation moves to the homophobia that some students see across the country based in the conservative Christian voting block. As the conversation evolves, eventually it turns more directly to the relationship between religion and the acceptance of homosexuality. One young Jewish woman and one young Black woman debate the viability of the Bible today, since passages in the Bible often guide faith-based positions: Is it an ancient text no longer relevant, or a text relevant to every age? Several young Black women and several bicultural students challenge each other about what some students see as broad-based homophobia in the Black community. But other students—White students and students of color—note that all cultures include individuals who are homophobic.

What becomes clear in this initial conversation—and what I try to help them understand—is that all of us are members of a number of discreet or overlapping groups in our lives: family; neighborhood or community; peer groups in and out of school; church, synagogue, or mosque. Some of these groups' values may conflict with the values of other groups. We all gradually learn to navigate these contradictions in our lives. But for many of these students, the challenges of accommodating contradictory values in the multiple groups and settings that are a vital part of their daily lives can be formidable.

Another semester the group is culturally mixed and includes a young lesbian passionate about issues tied to gay and lesbian lives. This group's initial discussion lingers on the power of stereotypes tied to gender and sexual orientation. The young lesbian is immediately taken with the identity development theories, proudly pointing out to the group where she feels she is within the stages. But she also describes lesbian friends whose situations are not so positive, and she shares with us the difficulty her relatives have in understanding the modern world of gays and lesbians. The students are talking about something that matters in their lives. We leave ready to read, outside of class, about gay and lesbian lives across multiple cultures in *Growing Up Gay/Growing Up Lesbian* (Singer, 1994), while in class we will screen the romantic comedy *The Wedding Banquet*, directed by Ang Lee (2004). Lee's film will take us to New York City and a young bicultural gay couple, one member of which initiates a convoluted situation involving a fake wedding to a female friend as a result of his reluctance to be honest about his identity with his parents, who live in Taiwan.

Lee's film, in my experience, is a wonderful film about gay issues for these students. The gay couple is bicultural, and the film is a romantic comedy that brings together two cultures and two sets of values; within the context of admittedly exaggerated comedy, it depicts the day-to-day life of a caring, long-term gay couple. Initially, some of the students are a bit uneasy with this matter-of-fact depiction of the young men's loving relationship and daily lives. But by the end, it has clearly left the students with an understanding of the very real pain for adult children, parents, partners, and friends that results when children—of any age—feel that they cannot be honest with their parents about their sexual orientation. It is a film that is at once warm, positive, funny, painful, and poignant—and very clear about the damaging effects of homophobia and heterosexism on the intimate, family, and social lives of good and loving people.

One of the strengths of the film is that its story not only gives students a broad understanding of the challenges gay couples may still face, especially in the coming-out process; it also enables them to relate to the characters simply as individuals, a couple, a family, or friends. In this room, the film touches gay and straight students from multiple cultures. One young White man noted that he could definitely sympathize with Wai-Tung, not because he himself is gay but because he knew what it was like to feel pressure from parents. A young Asian student was so taken with the range of issues in the film that she was going to recommend it to her family. For one bicultural student, the father in the film reminded him of a member of his own family coming to terms with learning one of his relatives is gay. In all of these ways, the film dismantles a sense of "other" about a young gay couple and brings such lives closer to these students' own.

Our text for the next few days is Bennett Singer's (1994) literary anthology *Growing Up Gay/Growing Up Lesbian*. I like the text for several reasons. Selections by gay and lesbian writers emerge from multiple eras and capture experiences in gay and lesbian lives across multiple cultures through nonfiction, fiction, and verse. The works explore experiences for GLBTs within an individual life, with friends, with families, with relatives, and with social and political forces that shape their lives. Many of the narrators of these stories—real or fictional—are like kids my students know; they feel familiar, and in that way we can diminish the distance between "us" and "them." In making the reading assignment for the students, I have marked some of the works with asterisks. The asterisks indicate that the stories emerge from cultures of color. I ask the students to choose any five selections in the collection to read and specify that three of those must come from the group with asterisks. That way, they will meet lives, circumstances, and attitudes related to sexual orientation in several different cultural contexts within their reading. Such freedom of choice is important. It enables individual students to look for the information they most need or are most interested in; in that way, the texts will take on relevance and meaning in their lives. Within the readings, they may meet, among many other lives, a young Black girl innocently discovering two women in a caring embrace and, after that, no longer feeling alone (Birtha, 1994). Native American writer Erna Pahe (1994) describes coming to terms with her lesbian identity both on and off of her reservation. A successful Chinese American woman in a poem by Kitty Tsui (1994) grieves for the fact that, because of her family's attitudes, her partner cannot be with her. Jesse Monteagudo's (1994) nonfiction narrative describes living a double life in Miami's Little Havana. And they may see a strong and loving White mother step forward and become an activist on behalf of her gay son (Manford & Manford, 1994).

Although this section of the course focuses on gay, lesbian, bisexual, and transgender issues, we have also met GLBT authors in other segments of the course. During the opening week, we have read several scholarly essays that give us helpful metaphors for approaching a variety of issues we will explore throughout the course. One is "Report from the Bahamas" by June Jordan (1995), a meditation on the factors that may or may not facilitate connections among individuals. Another is "La Güera" by Cherrie Moraga (2007). Moraga describes coming to terms with her identity not only as a bicultural Anglo Latina but also as a lesbian. For one young bicultural student, Moraga's story became a way of understanding multiple oppressions: "[Moraga] realized that although she had been hiding and denying part of herself [in embracing her Whiteness over her Latina identity], she still had another battle to fight [to embrace her identity as a lesbian]. But first she had to admit it to herself; she experienced oppression not only outside but inside her skin." In reading personal essays on socioeconomic class, the students have met Richard Rodriguez (1982).

In an always evolving curriculum, after exploring multiple lives and perspectives through *Growing Up Gay/Growing Up Lesbian* (Singer, 1994), we have also, some semesters, looked at one more scholarly essay, "Straight Is to Gay as Family Is to No Family" (Weston, 2007), about the ways in which emerging gay- and lesbian-headed families have altered the nature of long-term gay and lesbian relationships. Since many of our students know or come from gay- or lesbian-headed households, this text, too, speaks directly to these students. Another year, a documentary film, *Dangerous Living: Coming Out in the Developing World* (Scagliotti, 2005), gives us a look at GLBT issues across the world—and thus provides a larger context for the lives the students have met in this country.

With these readings and films in their background, we gather in student-led small groups to consider two questions: What has been hard for the individuals we meet in these essays, stories, and films? And what has worked for them? Overwhelmingly, the students are taken with the challenges all of these individuals face in coming out—especially to their families. One after another of the students go to moments that point to the difficulties for young people in a society that has stigmatized who they are. A number of the students also return to the phrase "That's so gay" and a re-seeing and re-hearing of the phrase in the context of these lives—what it means beyond, to some, seemingly jesting moments among peers. When individuals from each group share their small-group observations with the rest of us, I'm left with the power of these writers and filmmakers to bridge the distance between the lives of gays and lesbians of all ages, across multiple cultures, and these thoughtful young students in front of me. One young Israeli American woman wrote later that she was most taken with a letter from a young man explaining why he was afraid to come home to Colorado after the state had passed an antigay amendment to the state constitution: "I just read 'A Letter to Aunt Shelley and Uncle Don' from *Growing Up Gay* (Shepard, 1994). I found this letter extremely moving. After I read it, I wished that everyone in the world could read it." Many are stunned by the power of place and environment to alienate, isolate, and deny a full life to gays and lesbians. One student is taken with the strength it would take for gays and lesbians to confront the issues facing them, because those issues are tied to one's essential self and often come from one's own family and friends. For another student, "no one" should face these situations simply because of who they are. The films, readings, and discussions have taken these students closer to understanding and to empathy.

I see this most clearly on our last day on this focus. For this class, we turn to transgender lives and issues. These students are increasingly surrounded by images, circumstances, and stories reflecting the lives of transgender individuals. Students see news stories and photographs of a "pregnant father" (Trebay, 2008) and a story of a family rendered unusual only by the fact that one of the parents had become a transman (Kelley, 2008). Smith College admission material indicates that to be admitted, a candidate needs to "have been born a female" (Rosenberg, 2007).

We begin class by screening a clip from the documentary film *Middle Sexes: Redefining He and She* (Thomas, 2006) and then discuss a recent article from *The New York Times Magazine*, "When Girls Will Be Boys" (Quart, 2008), about a transgender student at Barnard and then Columbia. For the first 5 to 10 minutes, we watch as the camera in *Middle Sexes* takes us into the room of an 8-year-old boy in the rural Midwest. In front of the camera, Noah dances and twirls soft billowy scarves, then wraps them elegantly around his body and head. The little boy experiences himself as a little girl. We hear his mother, father, and stepfather speak of their love for him, their understanding that he sees and experiences himself differently than the little boy he has been born as or as his brother experiences himself. They speak of how difficult it is for him to face the questions and taunts that surround him at school or among his peers. They express their fears for his future, especially where he is growing up, a conservative area far from large cities that are more accepting of who this little boy is and will be. His mother, in tears, says, "[My greatest fear] is that someone will hurt him." We leave this thoughtful family and gentle, animated little boy and return to each other in our room.

The students are deeply moved by Noah and his family: the little boy's sense of who he is; the parents' wisdom in raising him; and the danger he, as yet unwittingly, faces. Their questions flood forward about both Noah and his family. One young White woman, yearning for a better world for young Noah, wrote later about these moments:

> After watching the short clip on the little boy who thinks he is a girl or at least completely acts like one, I realized that while I think the family handles the situation extremely well, I feel bad for him. And I know that most other people do as well. I mean he is so young and already deals with discrimination and weird looks from his friends at school. I feel bad for him because he doesn't understand why he's getting this strange feedback from people in his community. I assume his parents tell him nothing is wrong with him, which is true because nothing is wrong with him; he is just not mainstream in his gender identity, which is what makes other people uncomfortable because they don't know how to react to it. The truth is, though, they shouldn't have to react to it. They should accept it and let it be. At least that's how I would want it to be in a perfect world, but unfortunately our world is far from it; otherwise, I wouldn't feel sorry for this little boy.

Another year, a young White man wrote that the film had given him a whole new understanding of what it means to be transgendered. What lingered for him was that being transgendered is not a choice, and yet transgender individuals are perhaps more discriminated against than any other group we have explored in this course.

We turn next to their responses to the article "When Girls Will Be Boys" (Quart, 2008), about Rey, a young female who, by the time she became a freshman at Barnard College, had begun transitioning to a male identity. As with meeting Noah, the students are deeply moved by the complexities facing Rey. Their questions reflect their confusions and their concerns: about what it means to switch gender identity, about surgeries, about relationships; and the practical, social, and philosophical issues, described in the article, facing those surrounding transgender students in college—their roommates, peers, and college administrators, especially at a historically women's college. "What about Rey's needs?" "What about women who wanted women as roommates?" "Would he have been more accepted if he were a transfemale?" Because most of the students in this classroom will be taking their own positions on college campuses within the next few months, their questions and their emerging attitudes will have a direct bearing on the campus citizens they themselves become and the type of campus community they can build and support. And then, in this discussion, one student in the group describes losing a gay relative—how hard it was for that relative to find acceptance, and what it feels like looking back on that loss. The room is quiet. As we close, I show the students two articles book-ending our look at transgender lives and issues: One describes the recent murder of a young transwoman in Colorado (Frosch, 2009)—Noah's mother's greatest fear. The other describes a father who transitions from male to female and whose family of wife and two young sons remains close and intact—with his sons generating a new name for their father: "Maddy," a name that is, in their words, "half 'Mommy,' and half 'Daddy'" (Boylan, 2009), another possible outcome for young Noah or for Rey.

The film clip of Noah and the article about Rey have generated many questions, but overwhelmingly these works generate a softness—a palpable sense of empathy—in this room among this group of mostly high school seniors still putting together their own sense of who they are. We leave this segment of the course with lingering questions—and this softness—among us.

This segment allows students to write their third short analytical essay—this time looking at aspects of GLBT identity and: place, relationships, the ways in which GLBT individuals have responded to homophobia, or interpretations of gender within the context of sexual orientation. Additionally, at the end of the course, students consider ways in which sexual orientation—as one of several facets of identity—affects the ability of any two individuals or characters we have met in the last two segments of the course to build full and satisfying lives in this country—and the implications of their findings (Appendix B).

The students' written explorations of issues emerging from the GLBT community—in their ongoing journal entries, in two short essays, or as part of their longer final essay in the course—range from the power of surrounding values in homes and communities to hurt individuals or damage lives for a prolonged period of time to questions about institutional practices and policies.

From open awkwardness the first day, students have moved readily to thoughtful questions and discussions; and from there to seamless, respectful integration and exploration of gay, lesbian, bisexual, and transgender issues in their references to texts, films, or life around them in their ongoing discussions or through their writings. Their actions make clear the utter naturalness of a focus on GLBT artists, scholars, lives, or issues in the classroom, for all students—straight students and gay students, no matter where they are in the coming out process.

SUPPORTING GLBT STUDENTS—SUPPORTING ALL STUDENTS—IN THE CLASSROOM

The focus in this classroom on the lives and issues of gay, lesbian, bisexual, and transgender individuals is intended to support all students. Such study helps all students more thoughtfully navigate their world, and it helps GLBT students find an expanding base of support and understanding.

Our study attempts to address students' day-to-day experiences that may produce uncertainty, a range of feelings, yearnings, needs, and questions. Background readings provide answers to some of their questions through reliable facts and theories. Identity development models begin to demystify a less familiar identity. A list of terms helps students communicate more thoughtfully in this room and beyond, and current reports reveal the struggles many GLBT students of their own age face in their schools—statistics that my own students find shocking. Our studying a timeline of the gay rights movement makes clear the decades of challenges—as well as the victories—for GLBT Americans, and a list of famous gays and lesbians can help gay or lesbian students feel less alone and all students understand the breadth of the impact of significant gays and lesbians in history. A review of a recently published guide to colleges written from the perspective of the needs of GLBT individuals offers all students information as they make important choices about the next steps of their lives. Nestled in the corner of our room, shelves of books—works of fiction, nonfiction, photography, and verse—hold further reading about GLBT lives and issues for all students and provide additional resources for GLBT students, their friends, and their families.

As we move into works of literature and films, the stories of gay, lesbian, bisexual, and transgender individuals across multiple eras and cultures open windows onto lives and dismantle misinformation, inaccuracies, and stereotypes. Our study brings the lives of GLBT individuals closer to us and enables GLBTs to become less "the other." Our readings also bring significant gay and lesbian writers from the past into our forum, restoring to them a wholeness of identity that may have been partially or fully hidden in classrooms for decades, and giving back to all of these students the fullness of their American literary history.

Through respectful discussions—whether on our readings, films, or aspects of the students' own lives—students can gain a broader understanding of issues affecting GLBT individuals, the need for support for these emerging lives, as well as the wide-ranging perspectives of their classmates. Such conversations allow students to see these issues become the focus of serious study and give students practice in discussing controversial issues important in civic and political life. They also acknowledge and provide support for students navigating the challenges of moving daily among groups who hold contrasting perspectives on gay, lesbian, bisexual, and transgender lives and issues—whether in their homes, in their schools, among their peers, or in religious groups.

As young writers, students explore these issues in their course journals and apply their developing skills in analytical thinking and writing to GLBT concerns in formal papers, enabling them to see themselves as agents for thoughtful reflection and action.

Thus, through the multiple modes of our study, these students are beginning to replace uncertainty and hesitancy with reliable information and comfort in exploring GLBT lives and issues. We have come together—gay or straight—over sharing both our questions and our moments of discovery.

EPILOGUE

During our screening of *Dangerous Living* (Scagliotti, 2005) one year, I find myself thinking: It's a simple thing, really. We're helping kids put together pieces of the world around us. The pieces are confusing; the broken picture is confusing. The pieces don't always fit, but gradually some part of the picture is becoming clearer. And that way we can think about what's in front of us to make our own decisions, to build our own lives more consciously. It's a simple thing, really. But beyond our doors, it's not always so simple. Teachers and administrators are threatened or fired for less; conflicting perspectives tied to sexual orientation strain and divide friendships, families, religious groups, and voters.

But the needs to explore the lives and issues of GLBT individuals here have deep roots, and in my own life in the classroom they stretch back, long before. I know now, looking back, that my students were there before me. They were ahead of me. Given enough freedom, enough choice, enough trust, some were able to find part of what they needed. I watched as one gay student chose Willa Cather to present in a study of Chicago writers and made a presentation that included her cross-dressing in daily life and in an early role on stage. Daria was an out young gay woman of color. In her words, at birth her father had rejected her color, and in recent years her mother had rejected her sexual orientation. In one conversation in the honeyed light of late afternoon above Clark Street, she tells me her mother wakes her in the night waving the Bible over her body and screaming for God to take away the faggot demons. In one of her papers, Daria has written of suicide, of wanting to bury herself in a corner of a park she loves in the city. She keeps her writings at home, but she is afraid they will be found. "You can keep them here, in this drawer," I tell her. "They will be safe here." Later, I notify our counselor of Daria's vulnerability.

And students who asked of Willa Cather's (1905/2007) Paul in "Paul's Case," a spirited and sensitive young man in Pittsburgh who loved the arts and resisted contributing his energies to the gray and gloomy profile of industrial Pittsburgh. And the students said, "Is Paul gay?" And I didn't know how to answer—I who had never had this door opened on the writers I knew. These students were ahead of me, and they understood Willa Cather and her concerns more deeply and intuitively than I could at that point. I who buried the needs of this boy in commentary not about the loneliness of a boy who feels different, but about a larger society that does not care about the gentle and artistic among us. Another student writes a profile on a transgender friend for publication. "This is not only a good piece of writing," I tell the young author, "it's an important piece of writing; because if your friend had these questions, so do others, and your writing can help them." Another young writer writes a trio of love stories, one of them a love story between two young men savoring the joy of discovering each other. I write at the bottom: "You have done an exquisite job of exploring multiple types of love." One day, years after an exploration of Gloria Naylor's (1983) *The Women of Brewster Place*, a young man tells me: "I can't tell you what it meant to me when you taught *The Women of Brewster Place*. Two of the women were lesbians, and you talked about them as though they were any other women and theirs was just another form of love. My mother is a lesbian. My siblings and I were teased a lot. But in that room, the two women of Brewster Place who loved each other and made a life together were just two women who loved each other. You made it natural."

A few years ago, as a colleague and I were preparing to add the segment on gay and lesbian issues to a course initially taught as Issues of Race and Culture, we mentioned to one of the seniors that we were in the process of structuring a segment on issues emerging from the gay and lesbian community. "I wish we'd had that this year," she said. "It's really important, and you know it is just by walking up and down the halls."

But I was not there for all of the students who needed this kind of teaching. I couldn't be there without growing up a lot more myself. For us as teachers, even as straight teachers, who want to help our students more fully clarify their world, there is first a coming-out process for us and our teaching, a time for us to gain a necessary clarity and understanding to be able to move forward in our teaching in ways that can help a broader array of our students. For one young woman's questions, I was not ready. For that, it would take years of my own growing. And so I know I failed her. And there must have been others who yearned for such a space and time to find others in the world and others in the worlds of their readings who modeled aspects of the lives they were moving toward, who could be models, help them find themselves in a world at once beckoning and yet, as yet, unclear and far away.

CONCLUSION: A PLACE FOR GROWING INTO WHO WE ARE

Many gay, lesbian, bisexual, and transgender individuals have seen the world around them improve: the gains of the gay rights movement; increasing positive visibility in the media: television series, films, the *New York Times* wedding pages; flourishing gay, lesbian, bisexual, and transmale- or transfemale-headed families; Representative Barney Frank fighting back tears as he urged the House to pass the Employment Nondiscrimination Act (ENDA) so that "15-year-olds need no longer be afraid to go to school or young people working at gas stations need not fear losing their job because of who they love" (Frank, n.d.). But many risks and vulnerabilities remain, especially in schools. Harassment and violence against GLBT students continue to contribute to high rates of absenteeism and dropping out, as well as underachievement and overachievement. School boards and antigay activists continue to exert pressure and take actions against schools to prevent them from building in supports for young GLBT students. Gay, lesbian, bisexual, and transgender writers, history, and issues are not being broadly taught.

Is this a model for American schools that we want to hold on to?

The study in this classroom seeks to acknowledge and address what these students see, what hurts them and those close to them, what they wonder about. Such teaching supports lives—those of our own students, those whose lives encircle them, and those of the writers and artists we study. In this classroom, we are all visible—seen, heard, respected. I allow myself to wonder: If gradually, day by day, we could eliminate homophobia, even if just in this one school, would we also eliminate the need for a coming-out process? So that we all, simply, could grow up together into who we are.

CHAPTER 5

Writing for Self and Others, Writing for Life: Speaking to Journals, Making Art, Building Arguments

INTRODUCTION: WRITING AS A TOOL FOR OBSERVATION, EXPLORATION, EXPRESSION, AND ACTIVISM—THE FREEDOM TO WRITE/THE SUPPORT TO SUCCEED

I feel Rousseau hover over my shoulder as I look out over these students before me, believing that, nourished, unencumbered, these students will grow and expand, take delight, and curl their minds around the world. They will open into the light. Not every child in front of me is unencumbered; some have heavy bands around their lives, and they must twist and bend and turn to find the light. All of these students, though, have rich lives ready for the writing. They come to us full of stories and full of the questions that compel us to write. Writers of all ages have questions to ask; stories they need to tell; losses, betrayals, and violations of life they need to probe. As these emerge, our students will write them. If we trust them and nurture them, they will show us what they need to write.

The stuff of great literature is broadly the stuff of childhood: the rhythms of a language, the memories of a hand, the attitude of a father toward his son. Those are the shards of life that metamorphose into the great pieces of literature. The stuff of great literature is also the stuff of what young writers write. As Flannery O'Connor knew, "Anyone who survives childhood has enough to write about for the rest of his or her life."

What do students need to enable them to become the chroniclers of their lives or individuals who use writing to probe the large questions that encircle them? Young writers need what any writer needs: They need someone who believes in them, and they need someone who believes in the stories they tell, the arguments they create. A teacher's respect for the lives, the power, and the abilities of his or her students is what produces good writing. Students need to be trusted to tell the stories they need to tell and share the ideas they need to share—to find their passion, to experiment. Good writing is writing from the heart, going to the places that delight and hurt us. To be able to do that, students need to trust us and their environment. And so we need to create the conditions for them to experience the need to write and the joy of having written.

Students need time and space to write, the freedom to write what they need to write, and eventually, an audience who appreciates them. Our job as teachers is to support that process: to give them the time for introspection and observation, to give them freedom to explore aspects of human experience that are pressing from within for expression. Out of that comes the perfect opportunity to help them gain skills in the craft of writing. Once they believe in a piece of writing—and know that we believe in their writing—they understand the need to make it the best it can be for their audience. They need help in understanding how to do that, what to do to gain an audience they deserve. And for that, we will be their editor, we will be their coach, their other voice that believes in this fragile piece coming into being. For them we will be the safety net under the daring, high swings of writing.

The English classroom is a perfect place for writing. Students are surrounded by texts that can engage and transport them and conversations that can stimulate and reward them, confirming their strengths as observers of their world. Reading texts together that speak to their lives and their world gives students models for focus and form so that they can choose the way they want to tell their stories, raise their questions. Reading is a stimulus to thinking about and then writing about the moments and issues that call us in our own lives and from the lives of others, that is, life around us. Engaging in or listening to their classmates' conversations about works of literature triggers memories, jostles emotions, gives them permission, prompts them to wonder and cast a gaze on similar circumstances in their own lives. Such conversations invite a look inside and a look around—the journey most writers must take: into the settings, the individuals, the relationships, the moments and the glimpses of the surrounding world that made a childhood, that made a child.

What happens when we trust and support these students as they write for themselves and others? What happens as they speak to a journal, make art, or build arguments—to reflect, to sort through the confusions of a life, to dazzle and to move with their designs, or to urge action in the real world around them? What happens as they move from the more private forms for understanding the self and the world, to art forms that shape stories and capture a world, and to forms of persuasion that take their own ideas public or rally others to get engaged in the pressing issues that surround us? We engage in what Hilma Wolitzer (2001) has called "embarking together on solitary journeys" (p. 263). In this manner, students become writers.

In the pages that follow, we will see the work of juniors and seniors in the semester-long elective Issues of Race, Class, Gender, and Sexual Orientation as they write primarily for the self in their course journals (Appendix B). We will see the work of freshmen in the year-long required course Reading and Writing Across the Genres: Self and Community as they make art

(Appendix A). And we will again see the work of juniors and seniors as they build arguments in analytical essays (Appendix B). Most writing projects in the freshman course are done in class, in a computer lab, where I can provide goals for each day's work and address questions and uncertainties as they arise; this enables me to support each of the students as they bring their work into being. Writing projects in the junior–senior course are done outside of class, although I am available to answer any questions that emerge throughout the process. Although one of the freshmen projects described here—digital nonfiction—relies on access to computers, all of the remaining writing projects need no more than pen and paper; their essence is writing as speaking from the heart and the mind. Additionally, although the freshmen write analytical essays throughout the year, here we will focus on their work as young artists.

With the advent of the Internet, all these students inherit a rapidly evolving landscape for writers, for forms of writing, and for publication. My own work with teaching writing, however, suggests that if students are given a good experience in working within multiple genres, in developing and trusting their own voice through both discussions and writing, and in developing an appreciation for structure, logic, clarity, and correctness of expression, they will fare well in this changing environment, making contributions to traditional forms as well as newly emerging forms on the Internet.

WRITING FOR THE SELF: SPEAKING TO JOURNALS

Most writing emerges from a need to write for the self and to write for others. Although all writing begins as writing for the self, the first audience, writers often yearn for a broader audience. Writing is always an interplay between the writer and another, even if that other is the listening and reading part of the self. Some forms, however, move more toward the self and some forms move more toward others. Journals often move more toward the self, largely serving the needs of the writer. Journals often reflect an act of thinking and speaking with the self. This makes journal writing an ideal form for reflection, raising questions, rethinking—engaging in dialogues with the self. Because a journal done as part of a course is often submitted to a teacher in one way or another, however, these dialogues with the self will be shared—with the teacher, an audience of one—and the writer knows that, and so they are simultaneously dialogues with the self and one other.

Here are the simple requirements for a course journal given to students the first week of Issues of Race, Class, Gender, and Sexual Orientation: In order to explore more fully the issues we will cover in this course, each of you will keep a journal throughout the semester. (1) You need to write a minimum of two journal entries each week. (2) Each entry must focus on an issue of race, culture, class, gender, or sexual orientation—from the class or course, school, neighborhood, city, or beyond. (3) Entries should be written in ink in the spiral notebook provided, or typed and inserted in the notebook. I will take up the journals every 4 weeks and comment on each entry, so that they may become a type of ongoing conversation between us. (4) Each entry should be approximately one paragraph long—but they may be longer if you wish (Appendix B).

What happens in these conversations with the self and with me? For these students, writing journals becomes a sustained opportunity to think about and write about aspects of race, culture, class, gender, and sexual orientation. Through their entries, they develop an ongoing relationship with writing about what matters to them. Their journal acts as a quiet companion. In their entries, they focus on themselves, their peers, their families, and their society, what fits and what does not fit. Sometimes they raise questions, sometimes they engage in problem solving, they try to order their thoughts, sometimes they reflect a new step of understanding, a movement toward some modicum of clarity. They use them as an alternative way of engaging in the course: responding to texts, films, discussions, and sharing ideas. In these acts they are engaging the self in exploration. They are readying the self for participation in society and preparing their voice for more informed participation in their public lives. In their journals, these students are, in the words of William Zinsser (1989), "writing to learn." In their journals, it's safe to ask questions, it's safe to wonder, to blame, to be lost. For journals to come into fullness, students have to trust that they can look at and share the self, the personal and the political.

Their entries are usually informal, unedited, often spontaneous, and, in their openness and candor, remarkably trusting. Some students engage in a sustained conversation with themselves and with me about a single issue: about thoughts that confuse or haunt them, about dynamics that they observe and little understand, about the treatment of others, about personal responsibility, about identity. Some write entries that are multiple pages long, some write formal essays, some create exquisite stories that teach in their meanings. Some carry their journal with them and write from other places. Taken from beginning to end, they reflect a personal journey. Often the students say goodbye at the end.

For me, the journals also serve multiple purposes. They offer an ongoing juxtaposition between the student's public and more private self—the self revealed in open discussions and in day-to-day life, and the self revealed in the relative freedom and privacy of a journal. They help me know students more fully, to see another side of them that may not emerge within the group. They give me a chance to engage in a sustained dialogue with each of the students about issues that are on his or her mind. Their entries give me some sense of their experience of the course: individual texts, films, discussions, group dynamics, teaching methods, and the impact of the course as a whole. They give me a fuller understanding of the impact of specific issues on students' lives and students' responses to them in order for me to continue to design a course to meet their needs. Their journals are always interesting, and they are often deeply moving in what they reveal of students' challenges and discoveries in relation to the complex issues that surround them. For both of us, the journal becomes a private dialogue.

What types of questions are on these students' minds? Is it okay to have prejudices if you know you have them and you know it's wrong? Why do people keep believing that America is a "classless society"? Why are men still considered superior to women?

Beyond questions, they describe moments that confuse them or they share emerging realizations: for a young Black woman, the excitement of voting for the first time; for a young Black man, the disillusionment that voting will never make a difference in his neighborhood, where all the young men he sees are, in his words, imprisoned in one way or another; for a young gay student, the loneliness of coming out.

Sometimes they write about issues close to them that they would rather raise in this form than in a group discussion. Here a young Black woman and a young bicultural woman give us stories that teach. Their stories are a glimpse into the fact that for many young women of color, Toni Morrison's (1970) exploration of the relationship between children of color and the concept of beauty in this historically predominantly White country in her novel *The Bluest Eye* is anything but fiction and "myth":

> "Look, she is so pretty, I want to be just like her." I will never forget the words of a former 3rd-grade classmate of mine. We were all sitting around the lunch table eating, and my friend showed us a picture of a young girl in the magazine. This little girl in the picture was White with blonde curls and blue eyes. My friend told me that she overheard some of her family saying that the only way you can make it in the world is by being White, and that White was the true beauty. At that very moment I had nothing to say. For all of my nine years, I had thought that I was talented and beautiful until my friend told me the "actual" truth.

> When I was about five years old I looked in the mirror and saw someone that looked like my mom; I saw a Latina. What I did not see reflected there was my White Irish dad.

"Mami, I wish I had blue eyes like Daddy," I told her one day. "But your eyes are beautiful," she responded somewhat hurt. "They are the color of my eyes and my family's eyes."

Growing up I have always loved the skin I'm in, but that has never stopped me from saying I am half Irish and proud of it.

I still have my mother's eyes, but I see the world through one blue eye and one brown.

As these students begin to understand the meaning of their own memories, observations, and questions, they can also begin to understand the meaning of these issues in national dialogues. To foster such thinking and writing for these young individuals helps them to gain practice in framing the issues that divide or hurt us as a nation and to begin to understand the importance of their gaining the confidence to take their thinking and writing about such issues into a larger arena.

WRITING FOR OTHERS: MAKING ART, BUILDING ARGUMENTS

All good writing starts as writing for the self, and often there is little clear distinction between writing for the self and writing for others. But most writers, beyond the shyness that often comes with a writer's sensibility, also want their work to have meaning for others, for it to serve a purpose beyond their own needs, and so most serious writers also write for others.

This requires creating a piece that matters to the writer, because if it matters to the writer, it has a chance to matter to others. For these students, beginning with their lives and experiences is consistent with producing the best writing. As they write the stuff of their lives, they are beginning to give order to confusion, to capture what has meaning. The power of choice each time we write invites them to write from the heart, the gut, the pressing human need to understand and to connect.

In this room we gain practice not only in writing; we also gain practice in sharing our work with each other. We learn what it feels like to hear others connect with what we or one of our friends or classmates has written; what it feels like not being alone, because a piece of writing from one person's world has spoken to a person in another world, and, out of that, what it feels like to be generous with one another.

Writing for others assumes an audience, a reader, a listener, and this makes it a more complex process and a process that makes the young writer more vulnerable. Compared to writing for the self, writing for others makes the writing more formal, and that necessitates within the writer an awareness of the presence of others.

And, as do most writers, young writers want their audience to appreciate their work. Therefore, their work must be clear, logical, and polished within a workable structure. The endpoint is not elements of form. The endpoint is the reader who, because of the writer's skill, can connect with the writer's world and out of that gain more understanding about human experience and the writer who gains the pleasure of creating a piece of writing that matters to him- or herself and to someone else. Telling stories, building arguments, writing is a form of power.

Each of these young writers making art—freshmen in Reading and Writing Across the Genres: Self and Community—and each of these young scholars crafting arguments—juniors and seniors in Issues of Race, Class, Gender, and Sexual Orientation—will move through several steps with each work: searching the self and the world; finding a focus; getting it down; having my response as reader and editor to elements of focus and expression as they are writing and after it has been submitted, and thus teaching elements of structure, logic, clarity, grammar, and usage in context; revising, polishing; sharing their work with others if they are willing; and holding on to it. Thus, each of their pieces will move to a polished copy with an audience. This is a snapshot of the writer becoming, a portrait of the artist or scholar as a young writer.

Through this process, these students will know the quiet pleasure of success and what made that possible. At times, their audience comes from my reading pieces to the class—with each author's permission. At times, it comes from the students reading their own work to others. At times, it comes from posting whole sets of vignettes, poems, scripts, or analytical essays or from screening each other's work done in the multimedia form of digital writing in iMovie. Even with this intent, however, in the flow of a year, there are times when works that should have had an audience did not, and thus, for me, something that might have been possible among us in the room was lost.

These students' inner lives, the stories they want to tell and the stories they need to tell, the arguments they need and want to make stretch far beyond what we can imagine for them.

Making Art: Writing Scripts, Poetry, Fiction, and Digital Nonfiction

How do we make art in this classroom?

All of our writing begins with reading. We read across genres, and we read across races and cultures. We read men and women, gay and straight writers. We meet writers whose worlds are worlds of plenty and writers whose memories are tied to want. In the freshmen course, we meet, among many others, George Bernard Shaw and David Henry Hwang, John Donne and Gwendolyn Brooks, Lewis Carroll and Sandra Cisneros; and, in a literary journey across the United States in short stories, we spend time with such writers as Hugo Martinez-Serros, Cynthia Ozick, James Baldwin, Willa Cather, Leslie Marmon Silko, Amy Tan, and Raymond Carver. For their last reading in the course, students choose a biography or autobiography. Thus, we nestle into plays, poems, novels, short stories, and nonfiction. We talk about them: what they describe for us, how they work, why they matter to us or don't. And then we write. We write for the stage: a scene, a script with one or two characters, with a beginning, middle, and end. We write poetry; we write character sketches, vignettes, and short stories; and we write brief autobiographical or biographical narratives (Appendix A). Given time and support, these diverse young writers, some of whose lives began on other continents, take us into their worlds; they go where they need to go; they use writing the way the best writers use writing.

Here we see glimpses of their finished work in scripts, poetry, fiction, and nonfiction—the distinct nature of their voices already apparent. Their writings take us from glimmers of childhood toward, and into, death:

They bring forward moments that hurt: "Are you some kinda Mexican?"

And moments that delighted: Coming home to a kitchen where "Papier mache chiles are fiery red/ and cover the kitchen walls on golden ropes."

Moments that are lived too much alone: "And Abby with her best friend Emma, competed on the swings/To reach the sky first and to the moon from there/But with all the playground activity around her/Fat, lumpy, Alberta Gwenny/sat alone."

And moments that frighten: the bum man on the sidewalk who stares.

They take us in front of a mirror in the yoga class: "She was heaving now. Her legs became Jello, her head grew to twice its size. The last thing Claudia remembered was the hippo in the mirror, pointing and laughing as she fell on to her soft mat."

They take us home—making necklaces from the flowers of the Huang-Ge-Lan tree in China: "'Huang-Ge-Lan necklaces, earrings and ornaments for sale! Only 50 cents each! Do you guys want them?' We looked at the anxious faces of the girls nodding, then at their huge baskets on their backs filled with grass for the pigs, down to their torn dirty shirts and pants covered with patches of cloth to mend the holes, and down to their straw shoes. 'You know what, you can have these for free,' I said. Dong Dong nodded, and stuffed the flowers into their tiny hands."

They recall even younger dreams than the ones that line their lives now: "'We can swing on the swing set every day!' Ari shouted. We sipped our juice boxes and smiled, planning that our lives thirty years from now would be no different from what they were right at that moment."

They show us the freedom that is childhood: directions for catching a frog, directions for mixing a potion to help Muhammad Ali with Parkinson's disease, and conversations with the fairies that cover a sister's bedroom wall.

And they show us the childhood that doesn't feel free at all:

> So there I am. Sitting. Watching. Waiting. When the bus door opens and in walks the mother and the son. They both have beautiful red hair, the mother's long and straight, and the son's curly and full of life. The boy's face freckled in all the right places. This was not the first time I had seen them, but this time the boy seemed to glow. His smile enough to brighten the dull black and blue bus, his laugh melting the frost off the window. Smiling he recited his ABC's. I knew it was wrong, but in my mind the alphabet never sounded so right. His mom smiled and corrected him, but I couldn't understand why. Why can't it stay the way he likes? Who says that there can't be four L's? Why does it matter that the MNOPQR and S are missing? Why does he have to learn the "proper way"? Why does he have to grow up?

They show us glamorous mothers, mothers who are there, and mothers who aren't.

They hold on to relationships that stretch—or break: A brother walking into the future. A helper leaving. The life of an autistic child and her distant father.

And they become poets in the face of history: "He led me to the wash-house/it was quiet as a tomb/'Mother, I'm taking my shower now!'/And mist filled up the room."

They know what aging eventually means:

> [Tata] tells me stories about her life in Colombia and all the struggles she has been through. Sometimes she's telling the truth, but sometimes it's her age talking. "Yo trabajaba con puerco todos los dias," she worked with pigs every day, she says. I think that is true. Sometimes she thinks her past is her present. She says, "Mi madre me habla," my mother talks to me. But we know that her mother is gone. Still, she holds the family together tight as if she's hugging us and will never let go. She keeps us standing as if the foundation of a building. But Tata scares us because we know better. We know what ninety-five years

and counting means. We know that this isn't where she wants to be.
We know that one day we'll call for her, "Tata, Tata," and one day
she won't answer, "Si, mihijita!"

They see an "old frail man sitting in a big, old chair."
They show us what time does, and how people die:

"It's teatime," [my Grandmother] says. I love teatime. All week I wait.
And finally, it's time. Today it's hot chocolate, spaghetti with mari-
nara, and egg salad. We love teatime, together. But soon teatimes did
not come as often. And the old woman stopped driving in the dark.
And our teatimes were shorter. And my sister was older. And nothing
was as it once was. There is an old woman, my father's mother. She
sits, as the green on the trees begins to turn, hands in her lap. And one
day she was not there. And then there was no teatime. For many days.
Many weeks. And many, many years.

Sometimes that death comes in the flow of a long life: "Gabriella could
even remember how her grandmother smelled. She could remember how
her grandmother would put Gabriella up on the counter to watch her cook.
These memories were killing her. Finally, she left her bathroom, climbed
over the dog, got into bed, and put a pillow over her head."
Or it comes in the form of a betrayal: "'Honey, hurry, we are going
to be late.' Susan then looked down. She was wearing all black and had a
little speech next to her. She quickly got up, grabbed her coat and headed
downstairs. Waiting to see her grandfather who told her he would never
leave her side."
And they show the trailing violence to the heart from those who die
young: "My best friend who I hardly remember talks to me in my dreams.
He takes me places I've never been and tells me stories I've never heard.
Sometimes I see images of my friend drowning. He is screaming, begging,
pleading for me but I cannot help him. And sometimes I cry for my best
friend who I hardly remember."
Sometimes, they even help another prepare for death: "I knew that
chocolate was the one thing Magic had never tasted since chocolate can be
deadly for dogs. So I cut a thick slice of cake and put it on a plate for him.
Later that afternoon we put him to sleep and I knew he was happy."
Sometimes their work shocks in its nascent sophistication, a voice remi-
niscent of Faulkner's—in the country, a wounded bird, an older woman, a
child. Or in its wisdom far beyond their years—about fate or timing, the
dull inevitability of a tragedy on an ordinary day: a lone garden gnome,

a bluebird perched on top of the oncoming traffic light—a distraction, a young life lost, an old one preserved.

And sometimes, it is clear that writing becomes for one student or another a constant companion to help them sort out the traumas that came far too early in their young lives. In piece after piece—as playwright, poet, fiction, and nonfiction writer—they go back and back and back to the same moment, the same scene, the same loss, trying to understand, trying to give it some kind of framework that makes it make sense.

For our last project, students write nonfiction narratives and then use those narratives to create short nonfiction films in iMovie. Students create an autobiographical or biographical narrative based on details they have gathered about one aspect of a life. Once that narrative is ready, they gather relevant images and sounds. All of these elements are laid into iMovie, creating brief nonfiction films with images, background music or sound effects, and their voice-over narrative. The last day of the course, students screen each other's films. These works, too, capture the staying power of certain moments in childhood: the remarkable gifts of the tooth fairy, the lingering questions encircling adoption, the awareness of a friend coming out. And for some, the dazzle of the famous: Stanley Kubrick nestled among the images and sounds of his films, Audrey Hepburn wrapped in glamour. We leave each other with these sights and sounds tied to each other's lives within us; they bring us pleasure, they touch us, they move us.

Given freedom, time, support, a rationale for correctness of expression, students become superb chroniclers of the human experience, its confusions and joys. Children are keen observers—they feel and see the patterns, the foibles, the inconsistencies around them, the gaps in logic. They, like all writers, use writing to respond to the world or reimagine it, remember, put pieces together, for themselves and others.

In sharing their work, they become guides for each other into the worlds they each inhabit. In reading their pieces to others, they create a space for us all. Burrowing into our human frailty, and the essences of our own lives, these pieces bring us together.

Their writings never lose freshness, and they constantly surprise. Sometimes, they also call on us to be watchful in ways that these young writers cannot be. Because students often write from the heart and because of human frailty, we must never lose sight of the real power of writing and the vulnerability of the young lives in front of us. Sometimes in their writing they show sides of themselves that contradict our public understanding of them. Sometimes what they show us delights. But sometimes what they show us means we must act. At times they may trust their audience too much. Even the most sophisticated and mature writers don't always have a full grasp of the implications of their writings. So, too, with young writers. Their trust, coupled with their needs, sometimes means that they are traveling to places in their writing that others may not be ready to understand or respect with a necessary gentleness. Students may also use writing to convey a most profound kind of aloneness; sometimes they use writing to tell us they want to die. At such times we have to protect these young writers from themselves.

Building Arguments

Engaging students in building thoughtful arguments that draw on multiple perspectives means helping them develop a crucial skill for active participation in a healthy, multicultural democracy. Here we see juniors and seniors in Issues of Race, Class, Gender, and Sexual Orientation building arguments that matter.

Throughout the course, students write four short analytical essays exploring aspects of lives and issues tied to race, class, gender, and sexual orientation (Chapters 2, 3, 4, and Appendix B). Their final paper asks them to go further.

The guidelines for the final paper are simple and open: Select one issue of race, culture, class, gender, or sexual orientation and, in seven or eight pages, examine the issue from eight different perspectives found in readings or films explored in the course. Students are expected to develop a thesis about the issue; house that thesis in an introduction that draws in the reader; prove the thesis clearly and logically step by step through points that support the thesis and through documented references to their sources using either MLA or APA style of documentation; and, as a result of that process, come to a conclusion about the issue, including implications for themselves as individuals and for this multicultural democracy (Appendix B). They may consult with me individually during any stage of the thinking, researching, and writing process.

Being able to develop and take a stand on an issue in a complex democracy requires preparation. It means reading broadly to examine a range of perspectives. It means thinking about those perspectives and, out of that, beginning to develop one's own perspective. Ideally, it means testing that tentative position in conversations and dialogues with others in a multicultural group—those who may share that perspective and, especially, those who may not. It means listening in those dialogues. And from that reading, thinking, discussing, and listening, it means developing one's own informed perspective to place before an audience.

Where students take this, as with all of the writing in this classroom, grows out of their own needs as thinkers and writers. Sometimes they pursue issues intimately connected to their own lives; sometimes the issues are ones that surround them. A few passages from their writing capture something of the range and nature of their thinking—and the emergence of a public voice. Their perspectives deserve an audience beyond a high school classroom.

For one young Black woman, Spike Lee used the power of art to urge all of us to re-see the choices around us: "In my eyes, Spike Lee's *Bamboozled* (2001) put the blame on us for not immediately seeing that minstrel shows still exist, that Black sitcoms are little more than modern day blackface and football fields and basketball courts are just contemporary watermelon patches, a mere setting for all people to guffaw at the past while tainting the future. We are all to blame."

For one young White woman, writers of color as well as gay writers help dissect the conditions that shape the construction of racial and sexual identity in America:

> Both race and sexuality are social constructions that limit and confuse American identity formation. The concepts behind them exist—there are people who have darker skin than others, and there are people who have different sexual desires than others—yet their construction to define and separate are simply ways to justify the domination of one American culture. And by naming a "normal" and an "outsider," thus is created a hero and a villain, and thus is constructed identity confusion. Sometimes, individuals can escape their otherness through assimilation into the dominant, straight, White culture, which may or may not be enough to make them feel American. Still, there is another solution that starts with American "society's various ethnic [and sexual] groups . . . develop[ing] a greater understanding of each other" (Takaki, 2007, p. 35). Without this, there is no way to turn otherness into likeness and history into something to be proud of.

One bicultural student opened up the broad implications of the poetry of Daniel Beaty:

> In Daniel Beaty's poem, "Duality Duel" (2003), he portrays the internal battle going on between the assimilating "Nerd" and the "Nigger." Whether dealing with race, class, ethnicity, or gender, stereotypes, expectations and shame play a large role in today's social climate. Some choose to live up to those expectations as a way of survival, others are either not able to or not willing. Their assimilated counterparts often denigrate them in order to boost their status. If we are to seriously look at these issues we must first deal with the dark and sometimes scary feelings of shame we feel in regard to race, class, culture, and gender in order to move forward. It is clear that failure to do so leads to a self-destructive road, because, how can we live a free

and meaningful life if we are not able to see worth in ourselves. We can't allow our actions to be controlled by fear.

The practice of reading, debating, researching, and—out of this—constructing a formal written argument fosters in our students a habit of engagement in significant issues and helps them develop a well-informed voice for entering public debate. It helps them develop a habit of engagement for thinking and writing about significant issues that affect the daily lives of individuals and groups in this nation.

Whether students are writing essentially for themselves or knowing that their writing will have an audience, the assumption in this classroom is that these young writers, their ideas, and their perceptions matter. As for any writer, their writing originates with need, curiosity to know and explore, and passion. They are figuring things out, writing to learn, writing to describe, writing to speak.

WRITING FOR A MULTICULTURAL AUDIENCE

The multicultural classroom provides a uniquely rich environment for the growth and maturation of young writers. Working with young writers in the multicultural classroom produces a pastiche of American stories and perspectives, an American anthology. Their writings become portraits of America, a chorus of American voices. Supported to tell their stories, to write what they need to write, their works reflect a broad range of American experiences and points of view that become the writing of a new generation to show us our world and help us understand it.

The multicultural classroom also provides a significant audience for an emerging writer's voice. Writers have the opportunity to speak about things that matter in their lives to those who may share their perspective and those who may not. They have the opportunity to say: This is important to me; this is what this feels like. They can express anger, hurt, or passion about what they care about. Segregated schools, tracking, and low levels of diversity in many schools and universities make such forums unusual.

Such a forum encourages a dual-path journey—into the self as a writer and out into the world as a reader of their writing to their audience. Their audience constitutes a small world, an environment in which these young writers can remember, describe, and reach out—to move, to make meaning, to make trouble, to make people see, to experience the potential and the power of writing.

Writing for a multicultural audience in the classroom can also help develop a writer's voice for a multicultural audience: an awareness, a sensitivity,

TOURO COLLEGE LIBRARY

a type of knowledge, especially when addressing or exploring conundrums of race, class, gender, and sexual orientation. Classmates' responses to their writing not only reflect the power of writing for public expression but may prompt within the writer a re-seeing, recasting, reimagining not only of the piece of writing, but of the self, through that sharing.

But writing for a multicultural audience is also complex. Because writer and reader are engaging in communication across borders of identity, a more complex relationship emerges between writer and reader as well as more opportunities for a failure to communicate effectively, a failure to understand each other, or a failure to connect. What do young writers need to think about in making art and in writing to persuade in the context of a multicultural audience?

There is from the beginning the sense of another, an "other" for writers, and this is broadened if the audience is a multicultural audience. Individuals in all groups start off a bit tentative with each other, but individuals in multicultural groups are coming together from starting points that may be less familiar to each other. The same tentativeness and awkwardness that may characterize cross-cultural conversations can influence students sharing their work with a multicultural audience. Such unfamiliarity means students can be more unsure of their classmates' responses, what will work for this audience and what will not. Writers writing for a diverse audience have to learn that their readers do not necessarily share their experiences, assumptions, values, and perspectives.

Multicultural audiences also create a more complex relationship among the identity of the author, the focus of the material, and the audience, based in the racial, cultural, class, gender, or sexual orientation identities involved in each. The relationship between author and reader can be strained if audience members feel that the identity of the writer has prevented him or her from being able to adequately create particular characters, dialogue, situations, or arguments. Young authors may not be sensitive to the nuance, meanings, and power of language across cultures or the borders of identity, nor do they understand the complex nature of the choice to create characters, dialogues, situations, or arguments that emerge from a culture, class, gender identity, or sexual orientation other than their own. A White student wanting to use dialect to create a character of color may easily alienate students of color in the audience; since the writer's classmates may not understand his or her intentions, the use of dialect may feel like cultural appropriation, or it may feel disrespectful and insulting. An Asian American student describing a Black character who frightens a young boy on the street may alienate Black readers in the class. Such instances point to the power and challenges of writing what we know versus what we are much less familiar with, as well as the difficulties of writing about the actual cross-cultural tensions and moments that divide us in daily life. As students attempt to create characters, language, and circumstances across lines of race, class, gender, and sexual orientation, they risk relying on stereotypes to guide them and creating wooden, remote, or offensive characters or arguments that offend rather than persuade. They may easily, even if unintentionally, produce elements of writing that have the effect of being racist, homophobic, or insulting in matters related to class or gender.

Most students do not have adequate experience with or an understanding of the particular challenges of effective communication, whether in speaking or writing, across cultural lines, and this means they can be uninformed, naive, and self-defeating in their use of words or images whose history and meaning evoke powerful responses across lines of race, culture, class, gender, or sexual orientation; or they may face particular challenges in how they frame characters and circumstances across these lines in words. In essence, they must learn how to write effectively about sensitive matters tied to issues and identity.

Given the challenges as well as the richness for young writers writing for a multicultural audience and the practicality of such a skill in this nation, what are useful strategies for them to know? How can we help students develop their voice for art or for persuasion—to discover the power of writing that works—in a multicultural world?

The first step in our students' writing for a multicultural audience is exploring texts and films grounded in multiple perspectives tied to cultures, class, gender, and sexual orientation. In this classroom we spend much of our time reading and talking about writers and artists from multiple cultures, classes, genders, and sexual orientations. Students see their own and others' lives and experiences reflected in what they read and screen. They see that both are the stuff of art and the basis for addressing significant issues in written arguments. They experience identifying with these writers' perspectives, and they experience needing to reach across borders to understand the worlds the writers and artists have created or what it feels like to have their own perceptions challenged or stretched as they are taken into less familiar worlds. I try to help them see that both are valuable experiences and that sometimes the most unfamiliar may be the most valuable. These readings and films in turn are an invitation to these young writers to write from their own lives, to write about what matters to them, and to understand the connections and the distances that may emerge between them and their audience based on the choices they make and the worlds they create as a writer.

As for any serious writer, young writers who wish to connect with a particular audience need to have a clear understanding of the purpose of their writing, and they need to have a sense of their audience. If they want their audience to connect with their writing, they need to ask themselves:

How might this passage or this story or this argument be read from multiple perspectives grounded in a broad range of identities? Writing for a multicultural audience, it is crucial for young writers to try to see characters, language, situation, and perspective from the point of view of both writer and multiple readers, and to balance this consideration with the need for them to write honestly about the human condition as they see and experience it. Just as each of them connects more with some texts than with others, some of their readers will connect more with their writing than will others.

For writers making art, if they are creating a world for their readers, is there integrity to the world they creating? Are these characters, their language, and their situations true to life? Are they authentic? Do they match a reality? Or do they fall into stereotypes, fail to take on meaning, fail to connect? Do they unintentionally alienate or insult through inauthenticity or what the reader experiences as the writer's troubling relationship to his or her characters, their language, and their situation?

For writers seeking to persuade through building arguments, what choices should they make to give accuracy and integrity to their argument and to reach their audience, draw them in, keep them engaged, and persuade them? How might their own perspective, assumptions, and language be experienced by readers coming to this text from diverse cultures, classes, genders, or sexual orientations? What is the historical relationship between the identity of the writer and identities of members of the audience, and how might that affect this communication? Does this young writer's text anticipate, acknowledge, and respond to the nature of his audience? For persuasive writing, are the writer's expectations, perspective, language, argument, and impact likely to be well received, likely to achieve his or her goal as a writer?

If these young authors want to try to reach across lines of race, culture, class, gender, or sexual orientation, they need to be aware of both their intention and their audience. In so doing, they have the opportunity not only to succeed in reaching their audience but also to connect with them in some meaningful way. If we are lucky in this classroom, reading the works of published writers as well as the works of the students themselves can acquaint the students with the power of writing, the power of storytelling, and the power of using one's voice in public on significant issues. It can bring them closer together as they explore the human condition. I can't help but believe that the stories and the arguments my students write, the works we hear from each other, bring us a step closer to understanding ourselves and to connecting us across the room, and across our worlds, with each other.

A PASSION FOR WRITING IN A DIVERSE SOCIETY

What choices in this classroom make it possible for these students to become such tender, vivid, and thoughtful interpreters of their world?

For freshmen, our writing always begins with reading and discussing texts relevant to these students' lives across multiple genres and cultures. The students see a variety of ways in which writers have drawn on their lives and told their stories. From the beginning, these students know they are respected and taken seriously as thinkers and writers. Each time they write, they will be supported to write from their own lives, needs, and perspectives; they will be encouraged to tell the stories they need to tell and build the arguments they need to make. Although I may talk with them about their own interests or concerns to help them get started, I will never tell them what to write. I am there to help them go where they need to go as thinkers and writers. They will experiment with writing scripts, poetry, fiction, multimedia nonfiction, and analytical essays, and some of those forms will be more appealing to them as individuals than will others. But all of our writing is done in the spirit of experimentation—of trying something out. We usually write in class—in a computer lab—within a relaxed and informal atmosphere, each student pursuing his or her own vision within a particular form. Some of them listen to iPods, quiet and focused within their own worlds. Teaching elements of structure, logic, clarity, grammar, usage, and documentation occurs within these workshops, either for the class as a whole or in conferences with individual students. Students know that they will be supported throughout the writing process, having their questions answered each step of the way; and they know they can expect to be given respectful and constructive responses in the evaluation of their work. They will be held to high standards. They will revise and polish each work, and each of those polished works will be saved—to be taken home in the spring, a record of a year of writing. With their permission, their works are often read aloud or posted. These students know that their work has meaning in this classroom and that one of the rewards of their writing is to see the pleasure that their work can bring to others—to all of us who share this space.

Juniors and seniors in Issues of Race, Class, Gender, and Sexual Orientation, working outside of class, explore a wide variety of issues of interest to them. Their explorations occur in course journals, four short essays, and one long essay. The focal points of their writing emerge from life itself, texts, or films. With any of their projects, students have the option of having individual writing conferences whenever needed.

CONCLUSION

These students, their inner lives, the stories they want to tell and the stories they need to tell, the arguments they need and want to make stretch far beyond what we can imagine for them.

How shall I say what they have written:

About not knowing how to tie a tie because a father has left.
About wanting to know a mother on the other side of the world and why she gave her away.
About angels who come to look after us when it's raining and it's late and we're alone.
And fat men who find their dreams and lose their lives in stories about circuses and wives who die.
About city streets with wedding carriages and a bum who sprawls across the alley.
About mothers who die and fathers who die and friends who die.
About a body in an alley, about two cousins shot one night.
About how maybe religion has outlived its usefulness because maybe it's at the heart of war.

I'll be leaving teaching in a few years, so I frequently ask myself: What's worked and what hasn't? I know that it took a long time for me to grow up enough to create a workable world in a classroom, to convert the anger of my own experiences with race and class in the segregated South into a useful power to serve the needs of my students, to see beyond the layers of confusions of my own childhood to create a space for the confusions of their childhoods. It took me a long time to understand the myriad ways in which our schools and our society have hampered the growing up of our kids, a society that equips some for success and for inclusion in the world of power but leaves others more or less to fend for themselves. They were way ahead of me, these kids I teach.

I am haunted by the unrealized potential of so many young writers in this society and by our national response, which has been to create a school environment marked by relentlessly hammering in and testing to disembodied skills rather than supporting teachers to foster and nurture in each of our students the abilities to read, to think, and to write from the unique voice that is their own as tools for communication, power, and connectedness in a multicultural nation.

In this classroom our work is both cyclical and outward. Reading and talking about the work of fine writers and artists across many borders shows us how to write; our own writings become our readings and the focus of our conversations; these young readers become writers, become speakers.

Dewey's (1916/1966) approach to learning—starting with the world and experiences and questions of the child—promotes writing from the gut, the writing that matters. He knew long ago what was essential for schooling young learners in this society. Critics of progressive education have taken much satisfaction in framing his work as a failure of rigor. But the anti-progressives have it wrong. Where many contemporary conservative educators go wrong is their assumption that in the progressive classroom there are ideals without the discipline and the development of skills necessary to achieve those ideals. Any ideal is worth little without the wherewithal to move toward it and grasp it. The multicultural classroom can be a vital and supportive space for the development of skills essential to the heart of a flourishing democracy.

The young writers I work with every day in the multicultural classroom have taught me about teaching writing. From their wisdom, these are 10 things I know about writing:

1. That all students, consistent with the good thinking of Rousseau, with nurturing and support, can grow and flourish as thinkers and writers.
2. That all of these students come into this classroom filled with stories and ideas.
3. That they need someone to believe in them, and they need someone to believe in their stories and in their ideas.
4. That they need the time, the space, the freedom, the guidance and support to tell their stories and share their ideas.
5. That the breadth of their thinking and writing is wider and deeper and more surprising than I can imagine.
6. That by imposing, by guiding too tightly, I will limit their flight, the vast possibilities of their wanderings, their curiosity.
7. That they deserve an audience.
8. That their writing shocks me in its freshness and breadth, in its depth and goodness and wisdom.
9. That when I read them, their writings move me, they take me to new places, they teach me, they delight me, they make me cry.
10. That learning to write effectively in this multicultural nation can give these students power. That sharing our writing helps us to know each other and to understand each other; that sharing our writing helps bring us together.

CHAPTER 6

A Multicultural Classroom:
A Real and Precious Community

INTRODUCTION

The high school class I look out over this morning is a real and precious microcosm of America. It's real because it reflects the tenacious social habits and pressures that pull apart individuals and groups in this nation, and it's real because it reflects the dreams and hopes that fuel all of these young lives. It's precious because our mix of students across the lines of race, culture, and class is increasingly rare in our divided society. And it is precious because it affords a stellar opportunity for students to build a caring, workable, multicultural community whose moments of shared learning will serve them well the rest of their lives.

My students and I are housed in beautiful buildings. We have all the resources we need, and more. But lingering American divisions flourish among us. We are in no ivory tower. Despite popular myths to the contrary, schools are never divorced from the outer world.

But the thrill I feel this morning is repeated, in some way, every fall and every morning as I enter the door into this small but vital multicultural gathering, because this group houses the dreams and possibilities of this country.

BUILDING A MULTICULTURAL COMMUNITY:
DEVELOPING HABITS OF THE HEART AND MIND

The multicultural classroom offers stunning opportunities for growth and exploration within and among students. It provides a space for individual exploration and growth as well as the opportunity to be part of a significant forum. It provides a safe space to learn more about the self, the lives and cultures of others, and the issues that impact our lives, through multiple perspectives.

This classroom is a place to bring students together to foster and forge a working multicultural and democratic community across the boundaries that separate us, one individual from another, one group from another—to understand the richness and advantages of our coming together; to fear our differences less; to know that coming together affords time to think and to learn, to share wisdom, for all of us to grow and flourish more than we can on our own. We are all potentially better for our being able to spend this time together.

Tentative Beginnings

Each fall and each spring, a new set of juniors and seniors enters this room to meet some of this country's most respected scholars and artists from multiple cultures and to explore together some of the nation's most vexing issues (Appendix B). This course is elected. All these students have chosen to be here. And each fall and each spring, the group of students coming together is unique. Usually the group is comprised of 30–35% students of color and 65–70% White students. In one semester, the group is White except for one student of color, and religiously diverse. In another semester, the group is approximately 50% students of color and 50% White students. Regardless of our mix, each individual will contribute uniquely to the group we create and to the community we move toward becoming in our shared days.

Consistent with the nature of group dynamics, as students take their places on their first days together, there is a tentativeness among them (Wheelan, 2005). They are uncertain of what to expect, they look at each other across the room, they are curious. Individually and as a group, they are new with each other in this room, even though some of them have shared buildings in this JK–12 school for as many as 14 years.

Also consistent with what we know about groups, their group dynamics will be among the most challenging there are because of the level of diversity represented within the group (Wheelan, 2005). Students enter this room carrying the unique experiences of their young lives that have shaped their values and perspectives to this point. And they carry the residue of daily shared lives in other courses, in locker rooms and halls, during lunch, and in school activities. Some have developed close friendships in the years they have been here. Some have experienced a distance growing out of lives that are not shared beyond the schoolroom door. Partly because of the nature of their lives thus far and the ways in which they have or have not shared their experiences in school, each student also enters this room and this group with a unique relationship to power and sense of self.

All these factors influence the ways in which they see themselves and others in the group. They affect their self-confidence and the degree to which they are comfortable sharing their thoughts and opinions with each other. Each of these factors will influence their individual experience of this course and the group and community they form while they are together.

Ups and Downs: Coming Together

The community building in this classroom has its origins in a shared purpose and shared activities as students work with scholars and artists from multiple cultures in texts and films, discuss those works, and write about them. The students are drawn into works that capture and reflect their own experiences and experiences that are very distant from their own lives but that affect individuals, families, and communities in this country in profound ways. Their daily readings or films mean that each of the students is constantly gaining new information and new perspectives. This in turn stretches their knowledge and challenges their assumptions in an ongoing process.

Their discussions give them opportunities to respond to the readings and films, share their perspectives, test their ideas, and develop their voices. They have an opportunity to see and hear each other's responses. They see each other's passions, uncertainties, needs, and hurts as texts and films trigger thinking about situations that may be very near to their own concerns or at a further remove. In the course of these conversations about always complex and sensitive issues, there are, in addition to the students' ongoing engagement or animation, moments of quiet or shared anger, frustration, and vulnerability. And so, as teachers, we must look out for each individual and for the group as a whole.

Turning Points

Consistent also with theories of group dynamics (Wheelan, 2005), there emerges within the course of these discussions one or more key discussions that strain these students' ties as a group but that ultimately deepen their relationships with one another. Such moments are grounded in passionate disagreements about issues close to their lives. For one group, such a discussion is triggered one week by wrestling out the use and power of the "*n* word" and another week by pondering the rights of gays and lesbians to create families and adopt children. For another group, it's homophobia in Black communities. For a third group, it's a debate over the teaching of American history and the degree to which the histories of cultures of color—in this case, Latino American history—should be part of that focus.

In each case, the debate erupts spontaneously out of very real and antithetical perspectives of the students involved. On the morning of the discussion of the "*n* word," one student has used it as part of discussing a scholarly text that made use of the word. It becomes clear that this has not been easily accepted by the group—that students are reacting depending on their own experience of the word and its meaning in their lives. One White student has suggested that perhaps the power of the word could be tamed if it were used more freely. But another White student feels very uncomfortable about that notion, and students of color immediately counter the suggestion *to* use it with describing real moments in their own lives and in history when the word for them and for others has carried terrible weight and power. As tensions mount, I mention that I myself would not be comfortable with using it casually in discussions, since for me it is associated with too many moments of pain and violence in the segregated South where I have grown up. I cannot separate it enough today in this northern, urban, liberal environment from its origins in history and in the South. The room is quiet after my own observation, and, as we've reached the end of class, the students move through the door still debating the issue.

The crucial discussion about homophobia and Black communities emerges in the group that is roughly 50% students of color and 50% White and includes students very close to issues for young gays and lesbians. As we have just recently begun our discussion of issues emerging from gay and lesbian lives, two students engage in a heated discussion over the meaning and interpretation of the Bible in contemporary life. And this leads to a discussion of homophobia grounded in, in some students' minds, conservative Black churches. As the debate grows more heated, students of color divide into two groups—those defending their relationship to Black congregations that appear to others to be homophobic, and those rejecting the homophobia involved on the part of the churches—and their congregations—altogether. It is a difficult moment for the group and for individuals involved, especially since in this discussion some biracial and Black students end up alienating other Black students, and Black students end up alienating White students with close ties to young gays.

In the third moment, the group is roughly 35% students of color and 65% White. From the beginning in this group, there have been distances between a group of young activist women of color and a group of more conservative White males. Repeated disagreements often punctuate our conversations about a range of issues. The turning point comes, however, in a discussion of the teaching of American history. One of the voluble young women of color mentions that she feels she has to travel back to Mexico to gain any understanding of Latino American history. One of the young White males counters that courses already spend so much time on people of color and that U.S. history ought to focus on what's central in "our country's" history. The distance between the cohort of young women of color and the young White males grows palpably in front of us, and as students leave that day, the young women of color confer, disheartened, in one corner of the room. Not only do they feel defeated; they also feel that a good male friend—also a student of color—has not risen to defend their position.

I explain that their thinking is tied to crucial decisions about curriculum in American schools, that it is an important issue, and that their stand is important. What they may want to consider is strategy and the best way to forward their argument. Unfortunately, ongoing distances between their positions and the positions of White males in the class have led to a sense of defeat and the purposelessness of it all. They leave the room subdued.

In each of these last two instances, I myself have been ambushed by the moment. I have not understood the moment quickly enough as it has unfolded to be able to intervene in ways that might have helped the students understand the conflicted nature of their positions and how we might better understand the power of the moment. In thinking about the debate erupting over homophobia in Black communities and churches, I end up conferring with a colleague who is Black and gay. We have a long talk about gays in Black communities and churches, and he leaves with me a bundle of books, including *The Greatest Taboo: Homosexuality in Black Communities* (Constantine-Simms, 2001), a fine collection of essays by Black artists and scholars on these issues. By the time the students reconvene the next morning, I suggest that all of them yearn to do what they think is right, what they think is good and humane. But in moments such as this, they are caught among the conflicting needs and values of overlapping groups in their lives. Individually, each of them will gradually learn how to move comfortably among these groups, each of which is important in their young lives. This seems to make sense to them and we take the next steps, together.

In the instance grounded in the teaching of U.S. history, I feel I should have helped all the students understand what was unfolding earlier in the discussion, but that evening I realize that for this group—which has started the course by engaging in these issues with unusual animation—perhaps it would be helpful to return to some of the general guidelines we lay out for ourselves at the beginning of the course for discussing complex and sensitive issues, and I return, myself, to the thinking of Ronald Takaki. As class begins the next day, I tell them that I was very moved by what had unfolded and that it points to a central issue facing American schools today: what should be taught and why. I help them understand that what they have confronted is a major issue that has deeply divided scholars and educators in recent years; that it is a question that fuels much debate and that this debate will continue; and that, as they find themselves in such debates, they may want to consider strategy: What choices might they make in the middle of such diverging perspectives and opinions in order to best serve their own position? Sometimes continued debate is effective and sometimes a strategy of quiet, in order to regroup, can be more effective—that is, to decide on the manner of pursuing the point. We all need to remind ourselves that we come together bringing very different perspectives; we need to remain open listeners so that the dialogues can continue. Without the dialogues, we cannot move forward. I also explain to them that if I had been thinking more quickly, I would have suggested that Takaki, whom we have met in an earlier essay, has done significant work that brings together both points of view they are debating. In his *A Different Mirror: A History of Multicultural America*, Takaki (1993) makes a case that will accommodate the young White students' need for key aspects of U.S. history to be a focal point and that also embraces the need for including the histories of all of the peoples who have made the country what it is—the position of the young women of color. All of this seems to make sense to these caring and good-hearted kids. The distance remains between the young women of color and the White males who have taken a strong stand on this issue, but this relationship will surprise us all in coming weeks.

Again consistent with theory on group dynamics, although it is not readily apparent, in each of these instances, these complicated moments ultimately serve well the growth of the group. Theory on group dynamics tells us that when individuals experience conflict in a group and move on satisfactorily, such a process creates a growing sense of safety (Wheelan, 2005): We can disagree and move on together. Successfully navigated and processed, these moments can build more trust and closeness within the group. This was particularly apparent one semester. In the group that often divided along the lines of the subgroups of activist women of color and several more conservative White males, a few weeks after the divisive conversation on conflicting opinions about the requisite nature of a curriculum for teaching U.S. history in American schools, the focus is on two essays particularly interesting to many members of the class: "From 'Kike' to 'JAP': How Misogyny, Anti-Semitism, and Racism Construct the 'Jewish American Princess'" (Beck, 1995) and "What White Supremacists Taught a Jewish Scholar About Identity" (Ferber, 2007). This particular class is the last class of the day before an extended break, and a few students are missing. Students leading the discussions are also among those who felt strongly about holding on to traditional focal points in the teaching of American history. One of the discussion leaders is Jewish, another is Catholic. The conversation that ensues is one of the best, most vital and animated we have had that semester. All students are engaged, full of questions, and the leaders are open in their appreciation for the essays and their own lack of understanding of a number of the issues being raised by the authors: the origin of the term *JAP*, its continuing negative impact on college campuses, its relationship to relationships within Jewish families, and the complex nature of Jewish identity as secular or religious. In the midst of this discussion, the focus turns more broadly to religious identities and to divisions within religions. What becomes clear is that some of the young women of color—who are Catholic—are now aligning with the young Catholic leader of the discussion, one of the young men with whom they have sparred so openly about the necessity to include all cultures in surveys of American history, as they share perspectives on aspects of Catholicism. And Jewish students with widely diverging relationships to Jewish identity and to Judaism come together in a broad and vibrant conversation about the range of identities and divisions among contemporary Jews. The discussion is superb—I know it, and all the kids know it. It sends us out buoyantly into vacation and triggers many responses in their journals. It has caused them to re-see each other in this complex multicultural group. It has altered the dynamics of the group for the remainder of our time together.

Shifts in Power and Sense of Self:
Toward a More Equal Distribution of Power and Voice

Such moments have other effects as well on this group of young scholars. Individually they are each becoming better versed in significant American writers and filmmakers from multiple cultures, more informed, more understanding about multiple sides of issues that divide us. Such moments challenge their assumptions and necessitate their rethinking them—perhaps to confirm the rightness of their own position or to reconsider their position in the light of other points of view that have emerged so powerfully.

   Such moments also become part of other moments that begin to effect subtle shifts within individuals—shifts tied to their individual power and shifts in their sense of self. Research tells us that females and individuals of color may be more frequently marginalized in groups (Wheelan, 2005). In the groups in this classroom, some students enter with a history of occupying a powerful position in the broader school community. They have taken on roles of leadership, they may be known as successful students, they are "popular." Other students have led quieter lives in this community both in and out of the classroom. Responding to scholars and artists from multiple cultures and to cultural issues, however, requires different skills and knowledge, and this begins to realign the traditional roles students have occupied beyond this room. Some students have become accustomed to being rewarded and acknowledged consistently for their knowing the "right" answers in a course. In dealing with significant multisided issues across cultures, however, their knowledge base will have its limits, and often there is no specific "right" answer, but multiple perspectives. Students used to being acknowledged for having the "right" answers—especially if they are White—can no longer rely on that being the case. Students of color who have experiential knowledge of many of the issues these scholars and artists work with not only have a broad and intuitive understanding of the issues but are not willing to accept assumptions, grounded in White perspectives, that counter what they know. White students accustomed to being academic leaders in their classrooms are confronted with having their responses and understanding questioned in ways they have not experienced. And this can be very uncomfortable for them. Students of color, however, who often have a lifetime of experience in knowing the issues these writers and artists are dealing with, are in a position to become superb interpreters of these texts and clear and powerful discussants on these issues. Such shifting of power tied to a knowledge base is disorienting for students used to having unquestioned academic success and power in classroom analyses of texts and problems, and this can be openly disorienting to these students. The ground is shifting below them; they are no longer the clearly acknowledged leader in a particular academic discussion; they no longer can be sure of having the "right" answer. In this group, they no longer have an unquestioned position of power (R. Merrick, personal communication, n.d.). Additionally, students whose perspectives have not held center ground in courses find themselves clear and powerful interpreters of these texts and have emerged as leaders in discussions. They have taken on significant power in the group.

These dynamics in turn begin to alter the students' sense of self. Students accustomed to being bold leaders in classrooms now often must become broad and open listeners; on some level they must begin to acknowledge what they do not know and what that means to themselves, to others, and to their sense of who they are. And students whose knowledge and skills have not held a central position in classrooms begin to understand the breadth and depth of their knowledge—they begin to reframe how they see themselves and their position in the group. They come into a different understanding of their own knowledge and, out of that, experience the power and importance of their voice. As one young biracial student wrote one evening in her journal after such moments in a class discussion: "I will no longer be silent." All of these shifts in personal power and sense of self begin to redistribute and equalize power and voice within the group and to shift the nature of interactions within the group. Individuals and the group must absorb these shifts and realignments, and clearly that is easier for some individuals than for others. The ground is shifting under these students; they know it, but they are not quite sure what it means—and it can make them feel uneasy.

Such moments also result in shifts within the larger group as students align and realign with others in shared or conflicting positions. Such intragroup motion breaks up old alliances and frees up both individuals and subgroups to pursue fresh and independent thinking that marks a broadening of their own thinking, places a broader range of perspectives potentially into the group, and serves to enrich the experience for us all.

All these elements of group dynamics necessitate leadership in which we as teachers closely attend to the needs of individuals and the needs of the group (Wheelan, 2005). We do not want to lose anyone—we want the course, the thinking, the discussions, and the writings to reward each student in ways that support and promote individual growth, a greater understanding of each member of the group, and group cohesion. Such dynamics also point to the importance of a broad and inclusive curriculum for all students.

During the process of these daily cross-cultural discussions, students are also writing about these issues. Writing entries in course journals, a series of short formal papers, a midterm exam, and a longer final paper enable them to comment on moments unfolding daily in the course or life around them; sort out their emerging ideas and feelings; and analyze what they are reading, thinking about, and observing (Appendix B). This, too, develops their voices—and gives them practice in thinking about and executing thoughtful writing on multisided issues for a multicultural audience.

With each of the groups that pass through this course, each group unique, each richly diverse and complex, we land in a similar place. The difficult conversations among us do, in fact, on some level bring us closer together. They become turning points in our life as a group. In the weeks that follow tense and difficult discussions, there is a type of gentleness in the room, a greater ease and comfort, and we move animatedly and comfortably toward our last day together. The myriad moments the students have shared; the wide-ranging points of view they bring to the group; the power of the focal points and issues in their own real, day-to-day lives; the ways in which they have moved back and forth with each other, holding on to what is essential about their own perspectives but trying also to hear the perspectives of others, do indeed bring us closer together. Their final papers give them time to pull together their thinking on an issue of importance to them.

Toward Community

What has their time together resulted in? These students have a better knowledge of each other, of each other's values and perspectives, and of why those have come to be. They have become better cross-cultural speakers and listeners. They have shared disagreements and tensions and worked things out. They have surprised each other, formed alliances, disagreed, shifted alliances. They have moved apart, changed, come closer. They are ready to go forward more informed, more thoughtfully into their multicultural world.

On our last day together in this course, the students share thesis sentences and key findings of their final papers over a potluck brunch. They all take charge of their own thinking in their final papers—they go about investigating issues that have particular relevance for them, and they use the papers for real-world problem solving; the papers hold their own ideas, grounded in their own responses to an issue that they consider from multiple perspectives offered by scholars and artists from multiple cultures. Ultimately it is their own informed analysis of an issue that they care about. We leave each other as we have spent each day together: developing our voices, sharing our perspectives.

There is a palpable sense of our being here together to share ideas and to say goodbye. There is delight in our shared meal, bringing together favorite foods from households nestled in many different cultures; there is relaxed and animated discussion about the semester the students are just completing or about what comes next for these seniors. And then there is the cleaning up and goodbyes. I know in all of these moments we have shared that something has worked in our time together. It is something as tangible as the books and papers they carry. And it has brought us together and held us together. And now, we will miss each other when we go. Something we have done here has worked, day after day. As a teacher, the end of a course or a year always brings me a type of sadness, but in this course, it is also a bittersweetness—that I will miss so much these kids and their hearts and minds and the way they have cared, every day, about the issues that can so divide us. What a privilege it has been to be with them, and what hopes I have for the lives they will live. And, partly because of what I have seen of their ability to build a workable and sustaining multicultural community within this classroom, what hopes I have for the contributions they will make to the larger communities in their future.

IMPLICATIONS OF COMMUNITY BUILDING IN AN AMERICAN CLASSROOM

What are some of the implications of this community building in an American classroom? What can we understand of the process and its benefits, challenges, and gains?

Valuing the Individual

Emphasis on the histories, literature, films, and issues of multiple cultures, as well as the multiple focal points and perspectives represented in our readings, films, speakers, and discussions invite all students to identify with the learning process; this leads to a sense of belonging as well as a meaningful and often passionate engagement in issues of history and issues of the day that impact their lives.

In this classroom, there is an emphasis on each student feeling a sense of belonging; each individual's life experiences, values, and perspectives matter. Each student can feel: I am part of this group, this process. I am seen. I am heard. I am known. I am not invisible. I matter. I count.

Each student also experiences him- or herself as part of a diverse group, a colloquium. As students work out their own positions on significant issues in daily discussions and as they come to see themselves through the perspectives of others, they develop a fuller understanding of who they are.

From Isolation to Community

This classroom provides the opportunity for students to create and become part of a significant forum and, in so doing, develop habits of the heart and mind that can bring them together, lead them to discover the joy in learning across cultures, and give them skills to nurture and sustain a multicultural community.

In this room where such diverse lives intersect, students learn about themselves and each other; they learn how to care about the lives and perspectives of others, how to problem-solve, how to make things better. They learn how to hear voices from across cultures, classes, genders, and sexual orientations. They begin to develop group-mindedness.

Students' ideas and values are in the process of being formed; the students are tentative and at times uneasy; but the focus on the issues that often pull people apart ultimately helps bring us together. Through sharing their time and their ideas, students gain more comfort in being together. Most significantly, they learn how to build a thoughtful, animated, and trusting diverse community.

Challenges Within Individuals

Our students' coming to terms with these areas of their lives is complicated by the fact that all these students, in one way or another, are in the process of constructing and coming to terms with their own identities.

Not unrelated to the diversity of culture, class, gender, and sexual orientation surrounding them, these students face the inner challenge of coming to know, to judge, to craft, and to accept the self as they begin to claim their adult identity. They also seek to understand their relationships to those around them. Their sense of self is in flux. They have varying relationships to their own identity. They are figuring out who they are in the context of cultural identities, in the hierarchy of class divisions, and in the spectrum of gender roles and sexual orientations. Additionally, many of them experience a vulnerability of identity in a society that has for centuries simultaneously rewarded those who are White, male, heterosexual, and privileged as well as asserted clear and cruel judgments in countless ways on individuals of color, women, gays, and the poor.

Students' observations and choices reflect the nature of those strengths, insecurities, uncertainties, tensions, and needs tied to developing a sense of self. We see these students' inner thoughts—in course journals—and how those emerge or do not emerge in their conversations, and then we see their responses to those conversations. We see the contradictions that their thinking embodies and the gallantry with which they move forward despite a stumbling confusion. We see them asking us for what some of it means.

Most of these students are also readying to leave home in one way or another. They are making decisions that will determine the location, focus, and nature of the community that will provide the basis for the next stage of their lives. This is both thrilling for them and unsettling, and they bring the yearnings, uncertainties, and anxieties that are the effects of the often competitive nature of that process into the classroom.

Challenges Within the Group

All these factors make our coming together as a group potentially challenging. Our coming together can yield difficult intersections, stresses, and at times collisions. The students' real differences can lead to complex and unsatisfying interpersonal or group dynamics engendered by that mix.

Students are coming together from multiple cultures, with varying histories, values, customs, and assumptions and with multiple relationships to language. Students are coming together from families with considerable differences in power, privilege, and resources. The differences in their neighborhoods can be significant and can lead to strained communication and ways of relating, in school and out. Students bring into this room greater and lesser degrees of confidence about themselves and their ideas. Their relationship to their own identity can bring comfort and joy to some but uneasiness, uncertainty, confusion, fear, secrecy, and isolation to others.

As a real microcosm of American society, this classroom community reflects the ever-evolving social complexities, tensions, and divides—as well as the yearnings and dreams—that mark contemporary American life. It reflects the tugs, pressures, and habits that can divide us by race, by class, and by aspects of gender and sexual orientation, as well as the wishes to build a cohesive and caring community. These students' lives have already been shaped in part by the racism, classism, and attitudes toward gender and sexual orientation that have surrounded their young lives. It is in the face of these divisive pressures and their wishes to come together that we seek to build our multicultural classroom community.

But our microcosm is also precious. In this era of increasing cultural diversity and the resegregation of many of its schools, the diversity that defines our classroom grows ever more rare. By acknowledging and tapping into the power inherent in our differences in race, culture, class, gender, and sexual orientation, we can tap into the power of these students to create a vital forum, to teach each other, to broaden each other's ways of thinking, and, together, to begin to tackle the significant issues that surround us in this society. We all stand to gain if students can develop such skills.

Their challenges in coming together are significant. But because they are also young and open, smart and curious and generous, they will create by the end of our time together—as they have every semester this course has been offered—a closer, more responsive, and more thoughtful community of young learners. That doesn't mean that that process is always easy—or predictable.

Gaining Skills in Cross-Cultural Communication

One skill these students gain includes a movement toward more successful cross-cultural communication, a skill more and more essential in this multicultural nation. Research by numerous scholars in the field of cross-cultural communication tells us that effective cross-cultural communication involves intercultural sensitivity, an emotional component; intercultural awareness, an intellectual component; and intercultural adroitness, a behavioral component. Intercultural sensitivity is tied to individuals desiring to "understand, appreciate, and accept differences among cultures" and develops in stages from "denial" through "defense, minimizing, acceptance, adaptation and integration of cultural difference." Intercultural awareness refers to the "understanding of culture conventions that affect how we think and behave"; and intercultural adroitness embodies the ability to engage in successful intercultural communication (Peng, 2006, pp. 38–39).

In this classroom, although the students are not formally aware of this, they are engaging in developing skills in all these aspects of successful cross-cultural communication. Their wish to work successfully with their classmates supports their developing intercultural sensitivity. Their reading, seeing, and discussing texts and films emerging from multiple cultures across cultural lines with each other enables them to begin to understand something of the ways in which cultures affect our thinking and acting. And their daily interactions and dialogues gradually promote a growing degree of intercultural adroitness. They see in front of them what happens when they have successfully conveyed sensitive questions or observations, and they see in front of them what happens when they have not been as thoughtful or effective as they could have been in their speaking, listening, or actions. They are, as a result, beginning to understand what works in cross-cultural communication and what doesn't; and they are, every day, gaining practice in developing that awareness, knowledge, and skill. Such gains will serve these students well all of their lives—in further schooling, in the workplace, in social settings, and in their public spaces.

THE LARGER CONTEXT: LOOKING BACK/LOOKING FORWARD

Why are such moments in an American classroom meaningful? What is the larger context of these students coming together and constructing a community?

Looking Back:
Countering Shameful Periods in the History of American Education

This multicultural classroom counters segregationist laws and policies designed to control and limit the education of people of color throughout the history of American schooling and to render impossible the building and nurturing of multicultural communities in schools. Despite our historical record as a nation of immigrants, throughout that same history those in power held relentlessly to a notion of White dominance. One of the ways this was expressed and buttressed was through controlling access to education for those who were deemed non-White. Schools became contested grounds for gaining a foothold in America. Over the years, as African slaves, Native Americans, Mexican Americans, Chinese Americans, African Americans, and Puerto Ricans as well as immigrants from Ireland, southern and eastern Europe, and Asia attempted to educate their children, they were controlled in one way or another in ugly and recurring chapters of the history of American schooling (Spring, 2007). Such actions reflected policies and practices synonymous with national shame.

Whites in power have controlled the education of groups of students of color in multiple ways: attempting to wipe out a group's culture (Native Americans, Puerto Ricans, and Mexican Americans), attempting to replace a group's culture with the dominant culture (Native Americans, African Americans, Mexican Americans, and Puerto Ricans as well as immigrants from Ireland, southern and eastern Europe, and Asia), and denying access to education (enslaved Africans and, at times, Chinese Americans, Mexican Americans, and Native Americans). Immigrant groups have mostly experienced programs and experiences leading to assimilation into the dominant Anglo culture and the need to live in two cultures—one in their private lives and one in their public lives (Spring, 2007).

In one way or another, children of color were denied access to schools for White children. Laws made it illegal for African American slaves to learn to read and write; policies placed Native American children in boarding schools that systematically destroyed their attachment to their language, family, and tribal culture. Students of color were prevented from attending school with White students: the segregation of African American children throughout the South; of Asian American, Mexican American, African American, and Native American students in California under the California school code of 1872; and of Mexican children in Texas. In Mississippi, Chinese students were sent to schools for Black children. In California, Asian Indian students were sent to schools for Mexican American students, and separate schools were created for Japanese students. In the 1940s, Japanese American children on the West Coast were pulled from their schools and forced into internment camps (Spring, 2007). The disjuncture between these decisions and America's insistence on its embrace of democracy is a violent one: "On the surface it would seem strange that a nation that identifies itself as democratic should have such a long history of racial and cultural conflicts and would have adopted deculturalization policies. These seemingly contradictory beliefs have had tragic results . . . and represent a deep flaw in the unfolding history of the United States and American schools" (Spring, 2007, p. 8).

Despite decades of struggles devoted to desegregating American public schools, schools that reflect students divided along lines of race and culture continue to create the core of most students' experiences with learning. The vast majority of teachers, even in many classrooms with a majority of students of color, are White. In many classrooms, a biased curriculum and biased textbooks still render aspects of students' histories and cultures invisible and tell a lopsided and biased story of American history and literature (Bigler & Collins, 1995).

As I look out over my students today, I am aware that many of them come from cultures whose children, throughout an earlier history, were cast off from many American public schools, denied those educational resources, shunted into segregated schools with fewer resources, or placed in schools that forcibly sought to pull them away from who they were. Such long-running and broadly conceived policies and practices supported the learning and voices of some students at the expense of others. Our gathering today in this classroom and our learning from each other through listening to each other and reading about each other's lives and cultures could not have been possible in other times and places.

As today's students file into class each day, their country is in the process of a long-running shift in demographics. A national minority majority is expected by the year 2042 (Roberts, 2008); already, non-Whites are the majority in almost one-third of the country's most populated counties (Rich, 2007). How will the students who file through our classes in the next years experience and contribute to a nation in which no culture has majority status? Where will power lie, and how will the exercise of power be played out? A backward glance is a sobering reminder of the abuses of power in the hands of Whites. How much of that legacy will flow forward to haunt the nation? What will be the legacy of decades of abuse of power and abuse of minorities by Whites in positions of power? Gary Orfield and John Yun (1999), researchers for the Civil Rights Project at Harvard University, caution that Whites had best hope for leaders of color to be more generous: "The new white minority in the schools, which will eventually become a white minority in politics, can only hope that the non-white populations show greater regard for access by minority whites than white leaders did for them" (p. 26). One of our White students seemed to anticipate that such a transition, already under way, will not be without its challenges: "I think that one reason racism is so prevalent in the USA is that as minorities gain power and wealth, Whites look at it as a direct blow to their own class; to have an outsider be in the same socioeconomic bracket as them would be unacceptable."

Those of us who care about the education of children in America today must ask ourselves: What is the experience for all students—students of color and White students—in the multicultural classroom? How are we honoring and supporting the lives and experiences of students of color who will soon be the American majority, as well as those of White students who as adults will experience this historical shift in power? And are not many American schools still reflecting a movement toward segregation by both culture and class, resulting in well-funded schools for the powerful, poorer spaces for the poor, with attendant widely diverging rates of achievement, boredom, and dropping out?

What all of this means is that the multicultural classroom embodies the potential for realizing the American Dream. Students can come together in an atmosphere created to foster respect for each student's history, culture, language, and personal knowledge as well as each student's potential contributions to history, today and tomorrow. Together, we create a way of being and learning together in order to move beyond the decades of policy designed to close off sound opportunities for learning for countless families and students of color, to pull families away from primary languages and broader cultural moorings, to segregate students from their peers or even their families. Today, together in this classroom, we can gain the broader education that comes from all of us learning from each other: sharing and adding the knowledge of one culture to another in the richness and fullness of the growth of an individual and the growth of the group—circles and circles of cultures, cultures side by side.

Looking Forward: Reconceiving and Sharing Cultural Capital

The richness and implications of the multicultural classroom invite a re-conception of the nature and role of cultural capital. Learning in this multicultural classroom recognizes and honors the cultural capital of all students. Pierre Bourdieu's (1986) analysis of cultural capital—one's own embodiment of valued aspects of a particular culture, material objects, or educational credentials—suggests that capital associated with the dominant group has the most status in a society. As the capital of the dominant culture is reinforced in schools, such capital takes on more value, and the capital possessed by students from nondominant groups is valued less. The deficit model of evaluating student achievement has long noted the uneven cultural capital brought into a schoolroom by students from varying socioeconomic backgrounds. According to this view, students whose evenings and week-ends are filled with books and visits to museums and theaters are equipped with a cultural capital that is markedly useful in classroom learning and for succeeding in circles of power. These students, moreover, are held in contrast to those students whose upbringings have evidenced little to no us-able cultural capital to draw on in the classroom or that will allow them to enter the circles of power of the dominant culture. Thus, the deficit theory holds, certain students start ahead of others and there is little way in which those with little cultural capital can accumulate enough to match that of the privileged students next to them.

The problem with the deficit model of classroom cultural capital is the profound bias about wisdom and knowledge that lies at its core. All chil-dren walk into a classroom with cultural capital. But traditionally, many educators have chosen to recognize only certain types of that cultural capital because it was associated with the dominant culture. Such bias immediately privileges the privileged students and disadvantages those children whose cultural capital is different from cultural capital that embodies the effects of privilege—thus further entrenching the notion of what is valuable cultural capital and what is not.

To describe cultural capital as the valued assets of the dominant group simultaneously endows those assets with more power and desirability while marginalizing assets that in a multicultural world—where, in the United States, the present dominant culture will soon lose its majority status—is to undervalue, for all, the importance of the cultural capital brought into the room by members of traditionally designated minority cultures. In an era when minority cultures will soon constitute the majority in this country— and already do so in many heavily populated counties—it behooves edu-cators to consider the value of cultural capital transmitted in all families because knowledge and understanding of multiple forms of cultural capital will be more and more important for those wishing to interact successfully with each other or to assume effective leadership in a multicultural nation in which the dominant White culture has been replaced by a minority majority.

Many students may presently walk into our classrooms with an abundance of Bourdieu's concept of cultural capital, which indeed opens doors for them in circles of influence, and it is indeed up to all of us as educators to give all our students the range of skills and acquaintance with disciplines that will identify them as well educated. But we do all our students a disservice if we continue to assign power solely to the cultural capital of the privileged.

In this classroom, my students' shared cultural capital includes a knowledge of moving daily among two languages and two cultures, the power of family life and support, the uneven distribution of opportunity for children across city blocks, street life, life in housing projects, the truncated lives of so many Black men, friends dying from gang violence, police harassment, racial profiling, radically uneven levels of violence from neighborhood to neighborhood in a great American city, not being able to pay for a prom dress, cultural discrimination in a workplace of minimum wage, museums, the theater, and foreign travel. All these students have much to teach each other and to learn from each other about lives lived in America and the issues and concerns at their core. By recognizing, drawing on, and enabling our students to learn from each other the wide-ranging elements of cultural capital represented within our classrooms—the cultures our students embody: their histories, language, their artists, their writers; the singular knowledge that each individual embodies shaped by his or her own specific environments and experiences—we begin to provide a type of wisdom and knowledge to all our students that should prove useful in the years to come and that should, in fact, confer a very valuable form of wisdom to maturing adults in a multicultural society. In this space, students who have grown up in subsidized housing learn alongside students from affluent homes. Within a few months, several of these students—friends who bridge separate worlds, who share neither race nor class—will share the same New England college campus. One is interested in public policy, another in law. I have no doubt that each of them knows more and cares more broadly and will serve our nation better because they have known and cared about each other and each other's lives and perspectives. Perhaps had Supreme Court Justice Antonin Scalia been able to gain in his education a broader base of cultural capital, he would not have found it difficult to understand why a young man not being sought for any wrongdoing would run from police (*Illinois v. Wardlow*, 2000; "Judge Rules Police," 2000)—this in a country where the sexual violence in jail against Abner Louima and the killing of innocent street vendor Amadou Diallo—both committed by members of the New York City Police Department—played out on national television.

Although some theorists maintain that it is naive or romantic to assume that all cultural capital is the same, in honoring the broad range of types of cultural capital that our students bring into the classroom, we respond to the multicultural nature of the nation and we begin to equip all students with multiple forms of cultural capital that should prove useful in their futures: teaching traditional forms of cultural capital, but acknowledging the limits to that knowledge; acknowledging the value of coming to understand a broader form of cultural capital and supporting the sharing of that form of cultural capital. For my students, I believe that knowledge of each other's forms of cultural capital can be a form of knowledge and understanding that will better equip all of them for their lives in their multicultural society.

It is precisely a lack of honoring the cultural capital of those whose lives are lived out beyond a narrowly defined and traditional locus of power in this nation that has created, in part, myopic, shortsighted, self-serving, and dangerous choices and policies on a national level. What must happen to equip all of our students for the world they are inheriting and will soon be overseeing is to gain a knowledge of and a respect for each other's cultural capital. It is our responsibility as teachers in the multicultural classroom to ensure this takes place.

From Today into the Future:
Understanding, Building, and Sustaining Multicultural Communities

The community we establish in the multicultural classroom is an important step for the next steps of these students' lives and for their future communities. The nature of their learning experience is crucial in equipping students as they move from classroom to college campus or the workplace. These students are at a crucial threshold in their development. They are in the process of forming adult opinions. What happens in a classroom can make a difference in their lives and ours.

The authors of *The Source of the River* make clear the necessity of this kind of education: "All groups [of incoming students] appear to be relatively unprepared for the interracial and interethnic interactions they will experience in college" (Massey, Charles, Lundy, & Fischer, 2003, p. 158). Unfortunately, the meaning of their words moves well beyond the unfamiliarity or discomfort students may feel in a culturally heterogeneous community. The meaning of their words is also borne out in the darkest manifestation of that discomfort: incidents driven by bias or hate crimes. According to the Southern Poverty Law Center (2000), "Almost weekly, new reports of hate crimes on college campuses make the headlines": assaults on Arab students at the

State University of New York Maritime College in the Bronx, the beating of a Black senior by three White students at Brown University for being a "quota" who doesn't belong, an assault on an Asian American student at the State University of New York at Binghamton, homophobic vandalism targeted at a Harvard resident tutor, or a professor's support of the thinking of Holocaust deniers at Northwestern University. Among the reasons given: Some students, especially those from culturally homogenous suburbs, are unfamiliar with diversity, and they "react against it." Communication about diversity sometimes triggers violent responses. Affirmative action and identity politics trigger some hostilities. Interracial friendships inflame some students. Adjusting to being away from the familiarity of home, stress, and the combination of diversity and individual or group competition on campus also contribute.

Thoughtful curriculum and pedagogy in the high school multicultural classroom can ease the transition from high school to college or the workplace—and better prepare students for those settings—through supporting them as they learn about the history, literature, and issues tied to a wide range of self-identified cultural groups. As students get to know each other and gain practice with cross-cultural communication, the management of multiple perspectives on any given issue, and community building, they become acquainted firsthand with the types of cross-cultural experiences, tensions, and debates that may well be part of their college or adult life. One study at a diverse high school in Cambridge, Massachusetts, confirms the usefulness of a multicultural learning community prior to leaving for new settings: "Cambridge high school is helping to produce young adults who are ready to operate in diverse communities. This skill is critical to living in this society, particularly as many future economic opportunities will involve contact with people who are from different cultures and may hold different worldviews" (Kurlander & Yun, 2002, p. 7).

As the students in my own classroom move into their new communities and into the workplace, and as they continue to encounter the richness as well as the cultural complexities that are part of multicultural America, they will have a context and understanding not only for the challenges they may experience but also for the destructive acts they may witness or encounter or endure. But their background in being with each other, discussing cultural and cross-cultural issues on a regular basis, as well as their familiarity with multicultural dynamics—whether involving identities tied to race, culture, class, gender, or sexual orientation—should invite them once again into the practice of productive and thoughtful dialogues with their new classmates or colleagues and, from there, to move toward thoughtful action for sustaining a vibrant and vital multicultural community. An observation by one young White woman in my own classroom suggested that she has begun to appreciate the significant advantages that can accompany being able to live and learn among multiple perspectives: "As people leaving this sphere of safety soon, we must be ready to be able to study politics from more than one perspective. This task is, by its nature, more difficult than simply studying that which will never insult or surprise us. However, it is much more rewarding and much more progressive in terms of overcoming history and using it to our advantage. An important part of overcoming racism, sexism, and prejudices in general is overcoming fear of being insulted."

After completing her freshman year of college in California, a young Jewish woman spoke of an additional advantage of this approach to learning. On her campus, while other White students had difficulty accepting Latino Solidarity Day, seeing the day as separatist in nature, this student placed the event in the context of what she had learned of racial identity development theories and models and understood the benefits that could accrue from the event for Latinos and for the campus community as a whole.

The students in this classroom are being prepared not only to anticipate, understand, and navigate a range of dynamics, tensions, and issues tied to race, culture, class, gender, and sexual orientation, but also to engage in constructive thinking and action in response—that is, to take an active role in nurturing and shaping a rewarding and productive multicultural community.

Perhaps this young Latina, in her last writing in the course, most broadly embraced a perspective that the authors of *The Source of the River* (Massey et al., 2003) are hoping for each year as a new diverse group of freshmen come together on college campuses—and what all of us are hoping for as members of this generation of students take their places as young adults in our communities. Drawing on a wide range of skills developed in a multicultural classroom, she writes—and speaks—to us all:

> In studying the multitude of dimensions of individuals, I do believe that I gained a better sense of how individuals' lives can be affected by their race, class, gender, and sexual orientation in today's society. America *is* diverse. It can be seen in the many ethnicities and cultures that make up this nation. But as for a democracy, when citizens are held back for their race, class, or gender it cannot be defined as a society where all are truly equal. In the stories of [authors Julia Alvarez and Almas Sayeed], we see that things like race, class, gender, and sexual orientation remain defining factors that hold back rather than enrich. I believe that America can move toward being not only diverse but also a democracy. We have all been defined by what we are rather than who we are, be it for what we look like, what class we're in, what our gender is, and what our sexual preferences are. It takes reflection

as well as action for the citizens in this society to realize the implications of retaining structures that devalue others by taking away opportunities, resources, and power. America can continue down the path to a diverse democracy if we all realize that the ability to construct a full and meaningful life in the U.S. is the human right of all.

CONCLUSION

And so, here we are in this multicultural classroom in Chicago, glorious in our mix. The diverse nature of the students leads us to a stronger sense of self, identity, voice; recognition of others and their needs; inclusion; and a sense of our own and others' significance and power in the context of today and in the future. Through reading, screening films, discussions, and writing, we are growing adept at crossing borders. We are attempting to lay the groundwork for a more successful multicultural America than the one these students have inherited, indeed, than all of us have inherited. We are discovering what has been falsely handed down about each other, letting go of the stereotypes that have deceived us, and beginning to replace them with what's real and reliable. We are working out our differences, deciding what we are willing to see differently and what we need to hold on to and why. We are working out a community in which everyone matters, because every one of us has something significant to teach, and we've all become ready to learn.

References

Abderholden, F. (2008, March 7). *Group: Literature assigned in school "Child Abuse."* Retrieved August 23, 2008, from http://cbs2chicago.com/local/deerfield .censorship.debate.2.671746.html

ACLU. (2001, April 5). *Doing the math: What the numbers say about harassment of gay, lesbian, bisexual, and transgendered students.* Retrieved July 1, 2009, from http://www.aclu.org/lgbt/youth/11826res20010405.html

ADC Research Institute. (n.d.). The Arab-American community: Issues of concern. Washington, DC: American-Arab Anti-Discrimination Committee.

ADC Research Institute. (n.d.). Facts about Islam. Washington, DC: American-Arab Anti-Discrimination Committee.

Al-Qatami, L. (2004). Facts about Arab Americans. Washington, DC: American-Arab Anti-Discrimination Committee.

American gay rights movement: A timeline. (2009). Retrieved March 12, 2010, from http://www.infoplease.com/ipa/A0761909.html

American Psychological Association (APA). (2009). *Answers to your questions for a better understanding of sexual orientation and homosexuality.* Retrieved March 12, 2010, from http://www.apa.org/topics/sexuality/orientation.aspx

Amott, T., & Matthaei, J. (1996). *Race, gender, and work: A multi-cultural economic history of women in the United States.* Boston: South End Press.

Andersen, M. L., & Collins, P. H. (2007). Why race, class, and gender still matter. In M. L. Andersen & P. H. Collins (Eds.), *Race, class, and gender: An anthology* (6th ed., pp. 1–16). Belmont, CA: Wadsworth.

Andrews, S. (Director). (1994). *School colors* [Video]. Boston: PBS/*Frontline*.

Anyon, J. (2008). Social class and school knowledge. In L. Weis (Ed.), *The way class works: Readings on school, family, and the economy* (pp. 189–209). New York: Routledge.

Applebee, A. N. (1993). *Literature in the secondary school: Studies of curriculum and instruction in the United States.* Urbana, IL: National Council of Teachers of English. Retrieved March 12, 2010, from http://www.eric.ed.gov/(ED357370)

Austin, J. (2006, Fall). Slacker U. [Review of the book *Our underachieving colleges: A candid look at how students learn and why they should be learning more*]. *Independent School, 66*(1), 124–126, 128.

Beaty, D. (2003, April 14). *"Duality Duel" Daniel Beaty (Def Poetry)* [Video]. Retrieved August 21, 2008, from http://www.youtube.com

Beck, E. T. (1995). From "Kike" to "JAP": How misogyny, anti-Semitism, and racism construct the "Jewish American Princess." In M. L. Andersen & P. H. Collins (Eds.), *Race, class, and gender: An anthology* (2nd ed., pp. 87–95). Belmont, CA: Wadsworth.

Beemyn, B. G. (2006, May 19). *Autobiography, transsexual.* Retrieved August 23, 2008, from http://www.glbtq.com/literature/autobio_transsexual.html

Bendau, M. C. (Producer/Director). (1994). *Gangs: Dreams under fire* [Video]. Los Angeles: Telekinetics Productions.

Bigler, E., & Collins, J. (1995). *Dangerous discourses: The politics of multicultural literature in community and classroom* (Report Series 7.4.). Albany: National Research Center on Literature Teaching and Learning, State University of New York at Albany. Retrieved March 12, 2010, from http://cela.albany.edu

Birtha, B. (1994). From Johnnieruth. In B. L. Singer (Ed.), *Growing up gay/Growing up lesbian: A literary anthology* (pp. 18–22). New York: New Press.

Bonilla-Silva, E. (2007). Racism without "racists." In M. L. Andersen & P. H. Collins (Eds.), *Race, class, and gender: An anthology* (6th ed., pp. 91–97). Belmont, CA: Thomson/Wadsworth.

Bourdieu, P. (1986). *The forms of capital.* (R. Nice, Trans.). Retrieved July 7, 2009, from http://www.marxists.org/reference/subject/philosophy/works/fr/bourdieu-forms-capital.htm

Boylan, J. F. (2009, April 24). *"Maddy" just might work after all.* Retrieved June 9, 2009, from http://www.nytimes.com

Brantlinger, E. A. (1985, May). Low-income parents' opinions about the social class composition of schools [Abstract]. *American Journal of Education, 93*(3), 389–408. Retrieved August 23, 2008, from http://www.eric.ed.gov/

Brantlinger, E. A. (1993). Problematizing meritocracies. In E. A. Brantlinger, *The politics of social class in secondary school: Views of affluent and impoverished youth* (pp. 190–202). New York: Teachers College Press.

Brantlinger, E. A. (1995, March). Social class in school: Students' perspectives. *Research Bulletin of Phi Delta Kappa, 14,* 1–4.

Brantlinger, E. (2007). (Re)Turning to Marx to understand the unexpected anger among "winners" in schooling: A critical social psychology perspective. In J. A. Van Galen & G. W. Noblit (Eds.), *Late to class: Social class and schooling in the new economy* (pp. 235–268). Albany: State University of New York Press.

Brooks, D. (2008, July 29). *The biggest issue.* Retrieved July 10, 2009, from http://www.nytimes.com

Cady, J. (2005, May 25). *Censorship.* Retrieved August 23, 2008, from http://www.glbtq.com/literature/censorship.html

Cady, J. (2006, January 13). *American literature: Gay male, 1900–1969.* Retrieved August 23, 2008, from http://www.glbtq.com/literature/am_lit2_gay_1900_1969.html

California Department of Education. (2004). *California reading list: High School (9–12)* [Reading list number 13+]. Retrieved August 17, 2008, from http://www.cde.ca.gov/ta/tg/sr/readinglist.asp

California State Board of Education. (2007, October 24). *English-language arts content standards.* Retrieved August 15, 2008, from http://www.cde.ca.gov/be/st/

Cass, V. C. (1984, May). Homosexual identity formation: Testing a theoretical model. *Journal of Sex Research, 20*(2), 143–167.

Cathcart, R. (2008, February 23). Boy's killing, labeled a hate crime, stuns a town. Retrieved June 19, 2009, from http://www.nytimes.com

Cather, W. (2007). Paul's case. In A. Charters (Ed.), *The short story and its writer: An introduction to short fiction* (pp. 117–131). Boston: Bedford/St. Martin's. Original work published 1905.

Cavitch, M. (2004, March 1). *American literature: Colonial.* Retrieved August 23, 2008, from http://www.glbtq.com/literature/am_lit1_colonial.html

Chin, F. (1991). *Donald Duk.* Minneapolis: Coffee House Press.

Cho, M. (n.d.). *Margaret Cho—Korea/Asian chicken salad* [Video]. Retrieved June 23, 2009, from http://www.youtube.com

Cho, M. (n.d.). *Margaret Cho talks about race* [Video]. Retrieved June 23, 2009, from http://www.youtube.com

Coleman, E. (1982). Developmental stages of the coming out process. In J. Gonsiorek (Ed.), *Homosexuality and psychotherapy: A practitioner's handbook of affirmative models* (pp. 31–44). New York: Haworth.

Constantine-Simms, D. (Ed.). (2001). *The greatest taboo: Homosexuality in Black communities.* Los Angeles: Alyson Books.

Cooper, A. (2000, June 22). *High school football hero* [Video]. New York: ABC-News 20/20.

Court, A., & Arango, V. (Producers). (1998, December). *Children of the harvest* [Television documentary]. New York: Dateline, NBC News.

Dewey, J. (1966). *Democracy and education.* New York: Free Press. Original work published 1916.

Engl 3300 gay and lesbian literature. (1997, Fall). Retrieved June 9, 2009, from http://www.uta.edu/english/tim/courses/3300SYLL.html

Espiritu, Y. L. (2007). Ideological racism and cultural resistance: Constructing our own images. In M. L. Andersen & P. H. Collins (Eds.), *Race, class, and gender: An anthology* (6th ed., pp. 156–165). Belmont, CA: Thomson/Wadsworth.

Ferber, A. L. (2007). What White supremacists taught a Jewish scholar about identity. In M. L. Andersen & P. H. Collins (Eds.), *Race, class, and gender: An anthology* (6th ed., pp. 111–115). Belmont, CA: Thomson/Wadsworth.

Fox, J. (Director). (1999). *An American love story* [Video]. New York: Zohe Film Productions/New Video Group.

Frank, B. (n.d.). *ENDA: Barney Frank gets personal in debate's final speech* [Video]. Retrieved August 23, 2008, from http://www.youtube.com

Frank, D. (Ed.). (2001). *Francis W. Parker. Talks on pedagogics: An outline of the theory of concentration and other writings.* Chicago: Francis W. Parker School.

Freire, P. (1971). *Pedagogy of the oppressed* (M. B. Ramos, Trans.). New York: Herder & Herder.

Frosch, D. (2009, April 16). Murder trial tests Colorado hate-crime statute. Retrieved March 12, 2010, from http://www.nytimes.com

Frye, M. (2007). Oppression. In M. L. Andersen & P. H. Collins (Eds.), *Race, class, and gender: An anthology* (6th ed., pp. 29–32). Belmont, CA: Thomson/Wadsworth.

Garcia Berumen, F. J. (1996, Fall). The Chicano/Hispanic image in American film. *Harvard Educational Review* [Electronic version]. Retrieved June 16, 2009, from http://www.hepg.org/her/booknote/238

GLBTQ terminology. (2008, October 22). In *Creating safe spaces for all youth: Working with gay, lesbian, bisexual, transgender and questioning youth*

(Family Issues, Bulletin #4428). Retrieved June 10, 2009, from http://www.umext.maine.edu/onlinepubs/htmpubs/4428.htm#terms

Glennon, L. (2001). Yale: Reflections on class in New Haven. In P. Lauter & A. Fitzgerald (Eds.), *Literature, class, and culture: An anthology* (pp. 360–369). New York: Longman.

GLSEN. (2004, October 7). *New poll shows at least 5% of America's high school students identify as gay or lesbian.* Retrieved August 23, 2008, from http://www.glsen.org/cgi-bin/iowa/all/news/record/1724.html

GLSEN. (2009). *Shared differences: The experiences of lesbian, gay, bisexual, and transgender students of color in our nation's schools: Full report.* Retrieved July 1, 2009, from http://www.glsen.org/cgi-bin/iowa/all/library/record/2374.html

Greenhouse, L. (2007, June 29). *Justices limit use of race in school plans for integration.* Retrieved June 20, 2009, from http://www.nytimes.com

Haggis, P. (Director). (2005). *Crash* [DVD]. Santa Monica, CA: Lions Gate Entertainment.

Hamako, E. (2005). Mixed-race identity and student organizing. (Photocopy handout).

Hattendorf, L. (Director). (2008). *The cats of Mirikitani* [DVD]. New York: Arts Alliance America.

hooks, b. (2000). Coming to class consciousness. In b. hooks, *Where we stand: Class matters* (pp. 24–37). New York: Routledge.

Human Rights Campaign. (2009). *How do transgender people suffer from discrimination?* Retrieved June 19, 2009, from http://www.hrc.org/issues/1508.htm

Human Rights Resource Center. (2000). *Lesbian, gay, bisexual, and transgender rights: A human rights perspective. Introduction: Understanding lesbian, gay, bisexual and transgender rights as human rights.* Minneapolis, MN: University of Minnesota. Retrieved August 23, 2008, from http://www1.umn.edu/humanrts/edumat/hreduseries/TB3/intro.html

Hurst, A. L. (2007, August). Telling tales of oppression and dysfunction: Narratives of class identity reformation. *Qualitative Sociology Review, III*(2), 82–104. Retrieved August 23, 2008, from http://www.qualitativesociologyreview.org/ENG/volume7.php

Hurt, B. (Producer/Director). (2008, October 9). *Barack & Curtis: Manhood, power & respect/Examining Black masculinity* [Video]. Retrieved June 10, 2009, from http://www.youtube.com

Illinois State Board of Education. (n.d.). *Illinois learning standards. English language arts.* Retrieved August 15, 2008, from http://www.isbe.state.il.us/ils/ela/standards.htm

Illinois v. Wardlow, 528 U.S. 119 (2000) [Oral argument transcript]. Retrieved July 7, 2009, from http://www.oyez.org/cases/1990-1999/1999/1999_98_1036/argument

Jandt, F. E. (2007). *An introduction to intercultural communication: Identities in a global community* (5th ed.). Thousand Oaks, CA: Sage.

Jordan, J. (1995). Report from the Bahamas. In M. L. Andersen & P. H. Collins (Eds.), *Race, class, and gender: An anthology* (2nd ed., pp. 23–32). Belmont, CA: Wadsworth.

Judge rules police had right to stop man. (2000). Retrieved August 20, 2008, from http://www.Ispoa.org/caselaw.htm#RS

Kaldas, P., & Mattawa, K. (Eds.). (2004). *Dinarzad's children: An anthology of contemporary Arab American fiction.* Fayetteville: University of Arkansas Press.

Kayyal, S. (2004). Shakespeare in the Gaza Strip. In P. Kaldas & K. Mattawa (Eds.), *Dinarzad's children: An anthology of contemporary Arab American fiction* (pp. 197–206). Fayetteville: University of Arkansas Press.

Keating, A. (2007, October 29). *African-American literature: Lesbian.* Retrieved August 23, 2008, from http://www.glbtq.com/literature/african_am_lit_lesbian.html

Kelley, T. (2008, April 27). Through sickness, health and sex change. Retrieved August 23, 2008, from http://www.nytimes.com

Kurlander, M., & Yun, J. T. (2002, January). *The impact of racial and ethnic diversity on educational outcomes: Cambridge, MA school district.* Cambridge, MA: The Civil Rights Project, Harvard University. Retrieved August 18, 2008, from http://www.civilrightsproject.ucla.edu/research/diversity/cambridge_diversity.php

LaChapelle, D. (Director). (2005). *Rize* [DVD]. Santa Monica, CA: Lions Gate Home Entertainment.

LAMBDA GLBT Community Services. (n.d.). *Famous GLB people in history: You're in good company.* Retrieved July 1, 2009, from http://www.lambda.org/famous.htm

Langston, D. (2007). Tired of playing monopoly? In M. L. Andersen & P. H. Collins (Eds.), *Race, class and gender: An anthology* (6th ed., pp. 118–127). Belmont, CA: Thomson/Wadsworth.

Lauter, P., & Fitzgerald, A. (2001). Introduction. In P. Lauder & A. Fitzgerald (Eds.), *Literature, class, and culture: An anthology* (pp. 1–13). New York: Longman.

Lee, A. (Director). (2004, June 15). *The wedding banquet* [DVD]. Santa Monica, CA: MGM Home Entertainment.

Lee, S. (Writer/Director). (2001, April 17). *Bamboozled* [DVD]. Los Angeles: New Line Home Entertainment.

Lev, A. I. (2004). *Transgender emergence: Therapeutic guidelines for working with gender-variant people and their families.* Binghampton, NY: Haworth.

Linkon, S. L. (1999). Introduction: Teaching working class. In S. L. Linkon (Ed.), *Teaching working class* (pp. 1–11). Amherst, MA: University of Massachusetts Press.

Lipkin, A. (1999). *Understanding homosexuality, changing schools.* Boulder, CO: Westview.

Lipman, P. (2004). *High stakes education: Inequality, globalization, and urban school reform.* New York: RoutledgeFalmer.

Madrid, A. (2007). Missing people and others: Joining together to expand the circle. In M. L. Andersen & P. H. Collins (Eds.), *Race, class, and gender: An anthology* (6th ed., pp. 17–22). Belmont, CA: Thomson/Wadsworth.

Malamud, B. (1983). The Jewbird. In B. Malamud, *The stories of Bernard Malamud* (pp. 144–154). New York: Plume.

Manford, J., & Manford, M. (1994). Mother and child. In B. L. Singer (Ed.), *Growing up gay/Growing up lesbian: A literary anthology* (pp. 208–216). New York: New Press.

Martin, R. K. (2004, August 25). *American literature: Nineteenth century.* Retrieved August 23, 2008, from www.glbtq.com/literature/am_lit6_19c.html

Massey D. S., Charles, C. Z., Lundy, G. F., & Fischer, M. J. (2003). *The source of the river: The social origins of freshmen at America's selective colleges and universities.* Princeton, NJ: Princeton University Press.

McNaron, T. A. H. (2005, March 14). *Coming out stories.* Retrieved August 23, 2008, from www.glbtq.com/literature/coming_out.html

Mock, F. L. (Director). (2003). *Maya Lin: A strong clear vision* [DVD]. New York: New Video Group.

Monteagudo, J. G. (1994). Growing up gay in Little Havana. In B. L. Singer (Ed.), *Growing up gay/Growing up lesbian: A literary anthology* (pp. 161–165). New York: New Press.

Moraga, C. (2007). La güera. In M. L. Andersen & P. H. Collins (Eds.), *Race, class, and gender: An anthology* (6th ed., pp. 22–29). Belmont, CA: Thomson/Wadsworth.

Morrison, T. (1970). *The bluest eye.* New York: Washington Square Press.

Morrison, T. (1973). *Sula.* New York: Plume.

Nair, M. (Director). (2003). *Mississippi masala* [DVD]. Culver City, CA: Sony Pictures Home Entertainment.

National Association for Multicultural Education. (2001, January 18). *Criteria for evaluating state curriculum standards.* Retrieved August 21, 2008, from http://www.nameorg.org/resolutions/statecurr.html

National Council for the Social Studies. (1991). *Curriculum guidelines for multicultural education.* Retrieved November 22, 2009, from http://www.socialstudies.org/positions/multicultural

National Poverty Center, University of Michigan. (2006). *Poverty in the United States: Frequently asked questions.* Retrieved June 26, 2009, from http://www.npc.umich.edu/poverty/

Naylor, G. (1983). *The women of Brewster Place.* New York: Penguin.

NCTE/IRA. (2009). *Standards for the English language arts.* Retrieved June 20, 2009, from http://www.ncte.org/standards

Nelson, E. S. (2006, November 15). *African-American literature: Gay male.* Retrieved August 23, 2008, from www.glbtq.com/literature/african_am_lit_gay.html

New York State Education Department. (1997, February 27). *English language arts resource guide.* Retrieved August 15, 2008, from http://www.emsc.nysed.gov/guides/ela/pdf

New York State Education Department. (2005, May). *English language arts learning standards and core curriculum.* Retrieved August 15, 2008, from http://www.emsc.nysed.gov/ciai/ela/elarg.html

Obama, B. (2008, March 18). [Transcript: Senator Barack Obama's speech.] Retrieved June 10, 2009, from http://www.nytimes.com

O'Hearn, C. C. (Ed.). (1998). *Half and half: Writers on growing up biracial and bicultural.* New York: Pantheon.

Orfield, G. (2008, Spring). *Race and schools: The need for action* [Research Brief, NEA Research Visiting Scholars Series, Spring 2008, Vol. 1b]. Retrieved April 27, 2009, from http://www.nea.org/bare/13054.htm

Orfield, G., & Yun, J. T. (1999, June). *Resegregation in American schools. Full Report*. Cambridge, MA: The Civil Rights Project, Harvard University. Retrieved August 20, 2008, from http://www.civilrightsproject.ucla.edu/research/deseg/reseg_schools99.php

Ortiz Cofer, J. (2007). The myth of the Latin woman: I just met a girl named Maria. In M. L. Andersen & P. H. Collins (Eds.), *Race, class, and gender: An anthology* (6th ed., pp. 393–397). Belmont, CA: Thomson/Wadsworth.

Pahe, E. (1994). Speaking up. In B. L. Singer (Ed.), *Growing up gay/Growing up lesbian: A literary anthology* (pp. 230–234). New York: New Press.

Pakula, A. J. (Director). (1998). *Sophie's choice*. [DVD]. Santa Monica, CA: Artisan Home Entertainment.

Patterson, O. (2006, March 26). A poverty of the mind. Retrieved September 16, 2008, from http://www.nytimes.com

Peng, S-Y. (2006). A comparative perspective of intercultural sensitivity between college students and multinational employees in China. *Multicultural Perspectives, 8*(3), 38–45.

Ponterotto, J. G., Casas, J. M., Suzuki, L. A., & Alexander, C. M. (Eds.). (1995). *Handbook of multicultural counseling*. Thousand Oaks, CA: Sage.

Poston, W. S. C. (1990, November/December). The biracial identity development model: A needed addition. *Journal of Counseling and Development, 69*(2), 152–155.

Quart, A. (2008, March 16). When girls will be boys. Retrieved August 23, 2008, from http://www.nytimes.com

Rich, F. (2007, August 19). He got out while the getting was good. Retrieved July 23, 2009, from http://www.nytimes.com

Ripoll, M. (Director). (2004). *Tortilla soup* [DVD]. Culver City, CA: Sony Pictures.

Rivera, T. (1992). *And the earth did not devour him* (E. Vigil-Piñón, Trans.). Houston: Arte Público Press.

Roberts, S. (2008, August 13). In a generation, minorities may be the U.S. majority. Retrieved July 8, 2009, from http://www.nytimes.com

Rock, C. (n.d.) *How not to get your ass kicked by the police* [Video]. Retrieved September 16, 2008, from http://www.youtube.com

Rodriguez, R. (1982). *Hunger of memory: The education of Richard Rodriguez*. Boston: David Bodine.

Rosenberg, D. (2007, May 21). *(Rethinking) gender*. Retrieved August 23, 2008, from http://www.newsweek.com

Rosenbloom, S. (2006, September 14). Is this campus gay-friendly? Retrieved July 1, 2009, from http://www.nytimes.com

Rossier, N. (Director). (2004). *Brothers and others* [DVD]. Seattle, WA: Arab Film Distribution.

Salloum, J. (Director). (2005). *Planet of the Arabs* [Video]. Retrieved September 18, 2008, from http://www.youtube.com

Sayeed, A. (2007). Chappals and gym shorts: An Indian Muslim woman in the land of Oz. In M. L. Andersen & P. H. Collins (Eds.), *Race, class, and gender: An anthology* (6th ed., pp. 358–364). Belmont, CA: Thomson/Wadsworth.

Scagliotti, J. (Director). (2005). *Dangerous living: Coming out in the developing world* [DVD]. New York: First Run Features.

Sennett, R., & Cobb, J. (1993). *The hidden injuries of class*. New York: Norton.

Shea, R. H. (2007, May/June). New frontiers in fiction. *Poets and Writers Magazine*, pp. 36–42.

Shepard, T. (1994). A letter to Aunt Shelley and Uncle Don. In B. L. Singer (Ed.), *Growing up gay/Growing up lesbian: A literary anthology* (pp. 220–223). New York: New Press.

Singer, B. L. (Ed.). (1994). *Growing up gay/Growing up lesbian: A literary anthology*. New York: New Press.

Sogunro, O. A. (2001). Toward multiculturalism: Implications of multicultural education for schools. *Multicultural Perspectives, 3*(3), 19–33.

Southern Poverty Law Center. (2000, Spring). *Hate goes to school*. Retrieved March 15, 2010, from http://www.splcenter.org

Spiegelman, A. (1991). *Maus II: A survivor's tale: And here my troubles began*. New York: Pantheon.

Spiro, J. (1996, April). Three thousand years of your history, take one year for yourself. In T. Solotaroff & N. Rapoport (Eds.), *The Schocken book of contemporary Jewish fiction* (pp. 347–361). New York: Random House.

Spring, J. (2007). *Deculturalization and the struggle for equality: A brief history of the education of dominated cultures in the United States* (5th ed.). New York: McGraw-Hill.

Stephan, W. (1999). Prejudice: Theory and research. In W. Stephan, *Reducing prejudice and stereotyping in schools* (pp. 24–39). New York: Teachers College Press.

Takaki, R. (1993). *A different mirror: A history of multicultural America*. Boston: Little, Brown.

Takaki, R. (2007). A different mirror. In M. L. Andersen & P. H. Collins (Eds.), *Race, class, and gender: An anthology* (6th ed., pp. 32–44). Belmont, CA: Thomson/Wadsworth.

Tatum, A. W. (2005). *Teaching reading to Black adolescent males: Closing the achievement gap*. Portland, ME: Stenhouse.

Tatum, B. D. (1992). Talking about race, learning about racism: The application of racial identity development theory in the classroom. *Harvard Educational Review, 62*(1), 1–24.

Teacher suspended for running pro-gay editorial in school paper. (2007, March 21). Retrieved August 23, 2008, from http://www.advocate.com/article.aspx?id=39165

Thomas, A. (Writer/Director). (2006). *Middle sexes: Redefining he and she* [DVD]. New York: HBO Home Video.

Thompson, M. (Host). (2006, January 17). *Raising Cain: Exploring the inner lives of America's boys* [DVD]. Portland, OR: Oregon Public Broadcasting.

Trebay, G. (2008, June 22). He's pregnant. You're speechless. Retrieved August 23, 2008, from http://www.nytimes.com

Tsui, K. (1994). A Chinese banquet. In B. L. Singer (Ed.), *Growing up gay/Growing up lesbian: A literary anthology* (pp. 179–181). New York: New Press.

Unlearning Chicano, Latino, and Puerto Rican stereotypes. (2002). Retrieved December 1, 2002, from http://www.inform.umd.edu/EdRes/UgradInfo/UgradStudies/Orientation/EDCP108OUNI

Van de Ven, P. (1995). Effects on high school students of a teaching module for reducing homophobia. *Basic and Applied Social Psychology, 17*(1), 153–172. Excerpt retrieved August 23, 2008, from http://www.questia.com

Van Galen, J. A. (2007). Introduction. In J. A. Van Galen & G. W. Noblit (Eds.), *Late to class: Social class and schooling in the new economy* (pp. 1–15). Albany: State University of New York Press.

Viramontes, H. M. (1995a). The Cariboo Café. In H. M. Viramontes, *The moths and other stories* (pp. 65–79). Houston: Arte Público Press.

Viramontes, H. M. (1995b). The moths. In H. M. Viramontes, *The moths and other stories* (pp. 27–32). Houston: Arte Público Press.

Wadsworth, A. (2007, November 7). *American literature: Lesbian, post-Stonewall.* Retrieved June 9, 2009, from http://www.glbtq.com/literature/am_lit5_lesbian_post_stonewall,6.html

Waters, M. C. (2007). Optional ethnicities: For Whites only? In M. L. Andersen & P. H. Collins (Eds.), *Race, class, and gender: An anthology* (6th ed., pp. 198–200). Belmont, CA: Thomson/Wadsworth.

West, C. (2004). The necessary engagement with youth culture [Excerpt]. In C. West, *Democracy matters: Winning the fight against imperialism* (pp. 173–185). New York: Penguin.

Weston, K. (2007). Straight is to gay as family is to no family. In M. L. Andersen & P. H. Collins (Eds.), *Race, class, and gender: An anthology* (6th ed., pp. 343–348). Belmont, CA: Thomson/Wadsworth.

Wheelan, S. A. (2005). *Group processes: A developmental perspective* (2nd ed.). Boston: Allyn & Bacon.

Winfrey, O. (Producer). (2006, April 21). *The Oprah Winfrey show: Class in America* [Television film clip]. Chicago: Harpo Productions, Inc.

WLS-TV/Channel 7, Chicago. (2008, July 28). *Ministers push skipping 1st day of school in protest.* Retrieved March 12, 2010, from http://abclocal.go.com/wls/story?section=news/local&id=6292268

Wolitzer, H. (2001). Embarking together on solitary journeys. In *Writers on writing: Collected essays from The New York Times* (Vol. I, pp. 263–268). New York: Times Books.

Zinsser, W. (1989). *Writing to learn.* New York: Harper & Row.

Index

About the Author

Mary Dilg teaches English at the Francis W. Parker School in Chicago. She is the author of several articles on race, culture, and education and two previous books in the Multicultural Education Series: *Race and Culture in the Classroom: Teaching and Learning Through Multicultural Education* and *Thriving in the Multicultural Classroom: Principles and Practices for Effective Teaching.*